NUMEROLOGY
for beginners

KRISTYNA ARCARTI

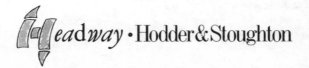

Headway · Hodder & Stoughton

For Beginners

This series of books is written for the growing number of people who, disillusioned with the sterility of our technological age, are looking to traditional, esoteric arts to find out more about themselves and others.

Other books in the series include:
Star Signs for Beginners
Tarot for Beginners
Palmistry for Beginners

British Library Cataloguing in Publication Data

Arcarti, Kristyna
  Numerology for Beginners. – (For
  Beginners Series)
  I. Title II. Series
  133.3

ISBN 0 340 59551 5

First published 1993
Impression number 10 9 8 7 6 5 4 3 2 1
Year   1998 1997 1996 1995 1994 1993

Typeset by Wearset, Boldon, Tyne and Wear.
Printed in Great Britain for the educational publishing division of Hodder & Stoughton Ltd, Mill Road, Dunton Green, Sevenoaks, Kent TN13 2YA by Cox & Wyman Ltd, Reading.

CONTENTS

Introduction   vi

What is numerology?   vi
A brief history   vi
People and numbers   vii
Lucky numbers   viii
Personalities   ix
What to do with the knowledge gained   x

Chapter 1   What are numbers?   1

Pythagorus   2
Later numerologists   4
Systems which link to numerology   5
The science   7
Looking at names   9
Finding a partner   10
Choosing a career   10
Numbers and colours   11
Planetary numbers   12
Working out fortunate dates   13
The meanings of the numbers   14

Chapter 2   Life numbers   15

What to learn from the birthdate   15
What you need to know to work out a life number   16

Starting to think about the science   16
The life numbers   17
Compound numbers   33
Predictions   43
Thinking of moving?   44

Chapter 3
Name and expression numbers   45

The 3, 6, 9 connection   45
Names and numbers   46
Finding the expression number   50
The expression numbers   50
Changing names   54
Business names   56

Chapter 4
Heart and destiny numbers   58

What are heart numbers?   58
The heart numbers   59
Destiny number   63
The destiny numbers   64

Chapter 5   Fadic numbers   72

How to find the fadic number   72
The fadic numbers   73
Working with the numbers   76

Chapter 6
Predictive numerology   80

Looking at years   80

The year numbers 81
Looking month by month 89
The month numbers 90

Chapter 7   Compatibilities   94

How to find compatibility ratings 94
Thinking more about numbers 96

Further reading   99

INTRODUCTION

WHAT IS NUMEROLOGY?

The science of numerology, the study of numbers, has been used for many thousands of years as a means of helping successive generations understand themselves and the people around them. In addition, as with astrology, numerology makes it possible to predict trends which will affect the future. To many people, it is nothing more than a fun game, to others it is a very serious science.

A BRIEF HISTORY

One of the earliest recorded instances of numerology being used in a scientific way comes from around 10,000 years ago, from the ancient Babylonians and Egyptians. It is, however, mainly to the Greeks and Hebrews that modern numerology owes its roots. The traditional meanings of the numbers come from interpretations going back to very early times, and some numerologists maintain that the science can be traced as far back as the dawning of mankind, when man first tried to understand the meaning of numbers and give them a spiritual or mystic significance.

Pythagoras, the Greek mathematician, astrologer and philosopher born about 580 BC, is one of the main sources of current systems and is recorded as saying that numbers are the first things of all nature. He held the belief that everything could be reduced to mathematical terms, and if expressed as a numerical value, the universe would be better understood. He founded a school on this principle.

The Hebrews, using what is known as the *Kabbala*, *Qabala* or *Cabbala*, formed a different system, but both ultimately translate letters into numbers. To the Hebrews, the process of relating words through calculation of their numerical values was called *Gematria*, and was a system employed many times in the Kabbala. There are several numerological systems and many numerologists will say that there is only one true system, the *Kabbalistic* system, all others being false. Other numerologists suggest that those using the Kabbalistic system only do so to confuse or imply more mysticism. However, I leave it up to the individual to use whichever system they feel is right for them, and make no judgements one way or the other. I personally use the western system, as the **22** letters of the Hebrew alphabet on which the Kabbalistic system is based do not correspond exactly with the western alphabet and must be transcribed, but you may feel more affinity towards the Kabbalistic system.

It is the numbers rather than the language that make systems universal, and the meaning of the numbers rather than the numbers themselves which is important. Everything has its own vibration, and that includes numbers.

People and numbers

John Lennon, it is said, had a fascination with the number **9**, feeling both his past and his present were linked to the number. As we will see, the number **9** is a very mysterious number, with unique qualities. John Lennon was born on a **9**th, as was his son Sean; many times he had connections with homes bearing the number **9**; the Beatles' manager, Brian Epstein, spotted the group in Liverpool on a **9**th; and their first recording contract was clinched on a **9**th. He met Yoko Ono on a **9**th, and it is said he felt convinced that the number **9** was important to him. He went so far as to include the number in several of his songs. It is interesting to note that his time of death, whilst being the **8**th in actuality in America was the **9**th back in Britain. The hospital at which he was pronounced dead was situated on **9**th Avenue, Manhattan. Many say that the number **9** is in fact the number of eternity, because of its indestructibility. Others feel that it is the number of the visionary. We will discuss this later on.

Many people hold firm to the belief that numbers matter in their lives. While not directly relating to numerology, it is interesting to note that, for example, two assassinated US presidents had a numerical connection. Kennedy was elected as President of the USA exactly **100** years to the week after Lincoln, and both had spent **14** years previously as members of the congress. There are also several other factors in the lives of these two men which match up, irrespective of the number factor.

Lucky numbers

There are many people who change their names, or the spelling of their names, for the different trend that the numbers can bring about, and many people believe that certain numbers are lucky for them. In Britain, many people think **7** is a lucky number, whereas in Europe, many countries think **5** is lucky. There is the well-known phrase, 'third time lucky', which seems common to many countries. Many people consider **13** an unlucky number, because there were **13** at the Last Supper (Jesus plus **12** Disciples, and of those **12**, one betrayed him). Those interested in tarot will probably have realised that in most, if not all, tarot packs, in the major arcana, the card numbered **13**, is death. **13** is not an unlucky number – to me it is quite the contrary. It is certainly a mystical number. Likewise, students of the tarot will realise that all the cards of the major arcana are numbered, and that there are **22** cards, mirroring the number of letters in the Hebrew alphabet.

By tradition, the number **3** is, as already mentioned, in addition to number **7**, considered lucky. If you look at all the numbers around you, birthdate, 'phone number, house number, age etc., there will always seem to be a couple of numbers which appear more often than others. To my mind, these are the numbers upon which you should focus, and which may also be lucky numbers for you.

At this stage it is worth pointing out that numerology should not be used to work out systems for lotteries, bingo or gambling. In these activities, chance plays a very large part and numerology does not allow for this. Studying numerology is unlikely to result in your finding a series of numbers which will help you to win large sums of money by chance.

Personalities

Character traits given for particular numbers are traits and not hard-and-fast rules. There is such a thing as free will, and often people will have changed facets about themselves with which they were not happy, or will have been forced to change because of pressures placed on them by others.

Some interesting points

Numbers have, to my mind, a life of their own on occasions. It is interesting to look at your own date of birth and work out forecasts using that alone. To show this, let's take a year, say **1940** and under that do a tabulation thus:

$$
\begin{array}{r}
1940 \\
1 \\
9 \\
4 \\
0 \\
\hline
1954
\end{array}
$$

There is a theory that states that to someone born in **1940**, the year **1954** would have had special significance, and if you go on from **1954** in the same way, the resultant year will again have had special significance. Try this out for yourself, and you will see the uncanny way that this really does work. It also works on historical dates.

What to do with the knowledge gained

You can have a lot of fun and learn a lot from numerology. You can look at your own life and those around you and work out character profiles for people, whether you have met them or not. In business, this can be quite an advantage, and many companies now look at numerology, as well as graphology (the study of handwriting), when taking on new staff.

You can use numerology to see when will be the best time for something important. It is said that Ronald Reagan consulted a numerologist before making major plans and there are several leaders in history who are reputed to have done likewise, Louis XVI of France and Adolf Hitler being just two.

Just as numbers came to hold a fascination for John Lennon, the same can happen to you. You may simply find it interesting to see how your character can be judged from your name and birthdate, and may also wish to check this against any astrologically derived information.

Ultimately, as Pythagorus believed, the movements of the planets, the changing seasons and the physical make-up of the human race are not determined by chance, but by mathematical laws. Learn these laws for yourself and you may find your life enriched as a result. It is very possible that some of your character traits will be highlighted, and you may wish to alter them in some way, the recognition of their very existence having been through numerology.

Numerology is fun, easy and yet scientific. It requires no psychic skills or extra talents. You don't have to be a mathematician to understand it; there are no complicated equations or formulae to memorise. Ultimately, however, you can learn a lot about yourself and friends, and from what you learn about yourself, you may be able to target areas for change or improvement.

CHAPTER

WHAT ARE NUMBERS?

*I*n this chapter we shall start to think a little about numbers, rather *than taking them for granted. As the book progresses, we will actually learn about transferring letters of the alphabet into numbers, what life numbers mean to us, and how we can learn about our personalities from numbers. We will also discuss the predictive side of numerology, discuss lucky numbers, fortunate dates, look at places and their numbers, learn more about the systems in use, and, hopefully, come to see numbers in a new light. We should also come to realise the close relationship between astrology and numerology, and its link with tarot. It is true to say that, for centuries, planets and signs of the zodiac have been given numbers. By the end of the book, you should be able to see the link between astrologically derived information and the information obtained from the numbers of your name and date of birth.*

Numbers are universal, their origin unknown. There are theories indicating that their foundation lies at the dawning of civilisation, but it is certainly true that many early peoples, Egyptians, Hebrews, Chaldeans, Hindus, and others, studied the science of numbers and wrote about their discoveries.

Where would we be without numbers? They are more than descriptive devices; they are a scientific necessity.

Numbers have a language of their own, which is not limited to boundaries but has a world-wide significance. The dictionary says that numbers are words or symbols which say how many. Numbers, however, go much further than that. Most of us have house numbers, telephone numbers; all of us have dates of birth and ages; many of us have bank balances showing plus or minus numbers; the size of a group of people is gauged by numbers, and so on. The need for numbers is immense.

Pythagorus

Pythagorus concentrated a large part of his working life on the study of numbers, to which he gave mystical properties. He is often called the *Father of Numerology* for this reason. As a result of his studies, he classified numbers into triangular ones (**1, 3, 6, 10** . . .) and realised they could be represented as a triangular array, and square ones (**1, 4, 9, 16** . . .) which form squares.

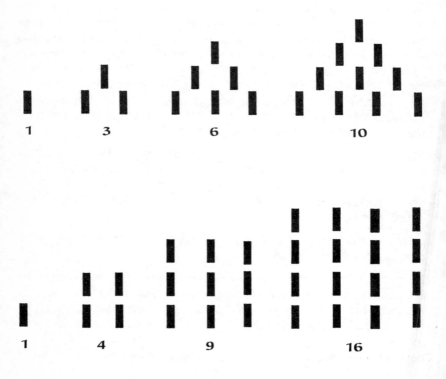

He also realised that any two adjacent triangular numbers add up to a square number.

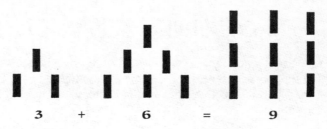

He formulated geometrical theories which are still learnt in schools to the present day. (Most people know, 'The square on the hypotenuse is equal to the sum of the squares of the lengths of the other two sides'.)

He also felt that each number had a personality of its own, that numbers contained the secrets of the universe, and that certain numbers were stronger than others. He suggested that odd numbers were powerful, **masculine** numbers, whereas even numbers were less strong, and consequently designated **feminine**.

It is said that he learnt about numbers from living in Egypt. The school of philosophy he founded on his return to Greece accepted only a few students, and he was very selective about who was allowed to benefit from his teachings. Tradition states that he allowed little to be actually written down (a link here with the Cabbala), his students being sworn to secrecy regarding what they learnt. As a result, many numerologists maintain that the confusion after his death regarding what he actually did and did not say, together with feelings that his teachings were 'the work of the devil', has lead to a complicated and vague system. I disagree with this, and feel that his system is far more easily assimilated by the general public than any other.

He strove to link philosophical thought with mathematics, and truly believed that numbers had great cosmic significance. He was a man seemingly far ahead of his time. He taught the importance of meditation and the effect that music has on the mind, and linked music and mathematics, something further expanded in the seventeenth century by the astronomer Kepler.

SOME INTERESTING FACTS

Many people since Pythagorus have studied numbers, and some people have made interesting discoveries, which despite the fact that they do not directly relate to numerology, are interesting all the same.

One such interesting fact which comes to light when you start thinking about numbers is the number of times the number **12** crops up. There are **12** months in the year, accordingly **12** zodiac signs; there were **12** Disciples; in fact, most religious leaders seem to have had **12** main disciples. There were **12** Knights of the Round Table, **12** Tribes of Israel, and so on. The times that number **12** occurs is amazing.

LATER NUMEROLOGISTS

During the times of the Renaissance, the philosopher Henry Agrippa devised a system relating mankind to numbers, and using a similar system, in the eighteenth century, Count Cagliostro, also known as Giuseppe Balsamo, devised a system from numbers whereby he could give prophetic readings. Both these systems are based on the Kabbalistic system of numerology. Like numerologists of our time, Cagliostro believed that transcribing the letters of a person's name into numbers gave a result similar to an astrological chart.

One of the most famous numerologists of this century was probably Cheiro (real name Count Louis Hamon). He wrote numerous predictive books and listed King Edward VII as one of his clients. For those who wish to read more about numerology than is contained here, I should point out that Cheiro often used numerology to try to predict the death of people. This, in my opinion, is not only unwise but unsafe, leading to severe mental anguish. Please bear this in mind should you be thinking about trying to predict such events.

Systems which link to numerology

The link between astrology and numerology is strong, in as much as each astrological sign has its own planet, which in turn vibrates to its own number. This is how this works out:

NUMBER	PLANET	RULER OF
0	PLUTO	SCORPIO
1	SUN	LEO
2	MOON	CANCER
3	JUPITER	SAGITTARIUS & PISCES
4	URANUS	AQUARIUS
5	MERCURY	GEMINI & VIRGO
6	VENUS	TAURUS & LIBRA
7	NEPTUNE	PISCES
8	SATURN	CAPRICORN
9	MARS	ARIES & SCORPIO

I have come across variations on this, for example that **6** is the number of Jupiter, ruling Sagittarius, but believe what is above to be the true number vibration pattern.

You may also notice that the sign for Cancer is in fact a **6** and a **9** next to each other.

In the major arcana section of the tarot, the cards are numbered, and it is not a coincidence that this is the case. The link between the two is so immense that those interested in the tarot and its connection with numbers are advised to read *Tarot for Beginners*, which contains all the information necessary to understand the two forms in relation to each other.

The strange number 9

Research into numbers can produce fascinating information. The number **9** is a fascinating number in its own right. If **9** is multiplied by itself, or any single number, the two figures which result will always equal **9** when added together. Try this out for yourself:

$$9 \times 6 = 54 \quad 5 + 4 = 9 \quad 9 \times 3 = 27 \quad 2 + 7 = 9$$

Keep going like this and you will see that the outcome is always the same.

Likewise, add together all the numbers from **1** through to **9**. You get the answer of **45**, $4 + 5 = 9$.

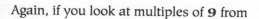

Again, if you look at multiples of **9** from

$$1 \times 9 = 9 \quad \text{to} \quad 9 \times 9 = 81$$

and add them together, the answer reduces to **9**.

If you take a row of any numbers, reverse their order, and take the smallest number from the larger, then add all the numbers of the answer together these will always reduce to **9**, for example **9432172 − 2712349 = 6719823**. Add these together, and you get **36. 3 + 6 = 9**. This works for any numbers you choose.

There are many more multiplications and patterns which feature the number **9**, and no other number is so 'magical'.

The science

Numerology as a science is relatively easy to learn, and even easier to use. The basic theory behind it is that every number reduces to a single digit, or **primary number**. The only exceptions to this are the **master numbers** of **11** and **22** which are considered to be special. One of the first and most important rules of numerology is that these numbers must not be reduced to single numbers, and if they are to be added to other numbers, again they must remain whole. The only exception to this is if the **11**th and **22**nd are birthdates.

From the numbers, we learn what are called **life numbers**, **expression numbers**, **heart and destiny numbers** and **fadic numbers**. An explanation of these and what they mean will appear as the book progresses, but at this stage, suffice it to say that **life numbers** (or **birth numbers**) show character traits, **expression numbers** how others see us, **heart numbers** how we feel inside, **destiny numbers** how we handle ourselves, and the **fadic number** our life's purpose, or what is sometimes called *karma*. We also have **compound numbers**, that is numbers of two digits, and again we will discuss this in greater detail as we progress.

There are also other things we can learn, for example how to use numerology for prediction and many other things which will help us in our lives, but we must initially see the codes to change the letters into numbers. So, let's now list both the Kabbalistic and Western systems of numerology.

KABBALISTIC SYSTEM

A = 1, B = 2, C = 3, D = 4, E = 5, F = 8, G = 3,
H = 5, I = 1, J = 1, K = 2, L = 3, M = 4, N = 5,
O = 7, P = 8, Q = 1, R = 2, S = 3, T = 4,
U = 6, V = 6, W = 6, X = 5, Y = 1 AND Z = 7.

Note: The number **9** does not appear, as the Hebrews felt it to be the number of God, based on their research which showed that the most mighty name of God must contain **72** letters, and $7 + 2 = 9$.

WESTERN OR PYTHAGOREAN SYSTEM

A = 1, B = 2, C = 3, D = 4, E = 5, F = 6, G = 7,
H = 8, I = 9, J = 1, K = 2, L = 3, M = 4, N = 5,
O = 6, P = 7, Q = 8, R = 9, S = 1, T = 2,
U = 3, V = 4, W = 5, X = 6, Y = 7 AND Z = 8.

You will notice that some of the letters of the Kabbalistic system remain unaltered in the western system.

The origins of both systems are lost in time. Some state that the Kabbalistic system is the older, others that the Pythagorean system pre-dates it. The facts are unknown. However, the earliest documents from the Kabbalistic periods of Jewish philosophy seem to be dated from around the thirteenth century, through to the sixteenth century, and on this basis, the Pythagorean system would seem to be older. Some numerologists will point out, to challenge this statement, that the Kabbalistic system is truly a Chaldean system, which takes it back further in time. No one knows for certain but the fact remains that there are two major systems.

As already stated, there are several other systems of valuation, some of which maintain that because there are four pairs of letters which correspond to single letters of the Greek alphabet on which the Pythagorean system is based, values for the combined letters of TH, PH, CH and PS should be used. Greek scholars will realise these correspond to *theta*, *phi*, *chi* and *psi*. The western or Pythagorean system given above is the most often used western system.

Looking at names

Having grasped the idea that you can change your name into a number, let's see how it works. Let's give you an example, and see what comes out. Remember that we are going to go into details in the following chapters on the meanings behind the numbers, so don't rush ahead without understanding the basic principles.

Let's take the name of *Paul Smith*. This is just an example. Paul doesn't have a middle name. Usually you use only the name by which someone is commonly known, but Paul doesn't have any other names anyway. If he had a nick-name or had been using an alias for a long time and that was the name by which he was most commonly known, we could also take that into consideration. However, Paul is just known as Paul Smith.

Throughout this book, it is important to realise that I will show all examples using the Pythagorean system. This is because I have a preference for this system, rather than for any other reason. Using the Pythagorean system, Paul Smith comes out as follows:

$$7 + 1 + 3 + 3 + 1 + 4 + 9 + 2 + 8,$$

This adds up to a total of **38: 8 + 3 = 11**. We do not reduce this further, because as we've already said, **11** is a **master number**. This number is therefore Paul's **name** or **destiny number**. Name numbers in themselves are only part of the equation, as names can be, and are, broken down even further. Let's just say at this stage, that **11** is a number connected to Paul.

As we go through the book, we will learn exactly what that means. However, we can assume from this, even at this early stage, that **11** will link with Paul in some way, that **11** may be lucky for him or that there may be another link where **11** crops up frequently in his life.

Now try your name, and see what comes from that, and, if you want, compare it to the Kabbalistic system to see what comes out from that.

Please note Whatever you do, remember that you cannot mix the Kabbalistic and Pythagorean systems. You follow either one or the other, not both.

finding a partner

A word at this point about compatibilities. Many numerologists would say that it is possible to work out compatibilities from the numbers found from a person's name and/or birthdate. This is quite controversial, and again may be rejected as unreliable. Later on in this book, however, we will examine compatibilities a little more. It is up to you to decide whether you wish to use these or not.

Choosing a career

Many people who are interested in numerology consult numbers to find a career, either for themselves or for members of their family. This is achieved by using the **life number** found from the birth date, and also by using the **destiny number** or sometimes also what is called the **personal number**. An example of this is that people who are number **5**s are often interested or talented in writing of some description, and so should be encouraged to look at this form of expression in their lives. Number **7**s are often politicians or active community leaders, and are often quite psychic, as are number **2**s. Number **9**s are very creative and are often found in the arts, film or stage. Further information on typical jobs for certain numbers will appear in the text at a later stage.

Numbers and colours

Let's take a look at colours. They too relate to numbers. The light from the sun's rays falls into **7** colours, and these are as follows:

red	**= 1** and **8**
orange	**= 2** and **9**
yellow	**= 3**
green	**= 4**
blue	**= 5**
indigo	**= 6**
violet	**= 7**

Colour can have a real effect on how we feel. Studies over the years have shown that people are far more relaxed in a room of one colour rather than another. Some people, for instance, will be happy in a yellow room (I have noticed over the years that Gemini people in particular love yellow or lemon rooms).

The studies linking colour and numerology all indicate that the number arrived at by adding together the numbers from the date of birth (which we shall later learn is the **life number**) and the number from the name (which is called the **destiny number**) is the colour most likely to have the best effect on overall mentality.

Let's take *Paul Smith* again. Let's pretend his birthday is 2nd September, 1956. His life number is $2 + 9 + 1 + 9 + 5 + 6 = 32$ which is further reduced to **5**. We have already established that his name comes out at **11**. $11 + 5 = 16$ which further reduces to **7**. We can therefore assume that violet is likely to be soothing to Paul, and he may well have a lot of violet in his clothes or surroundings.

Using this information, try to work out your own colour. Use the name by which you are usually known.

Planetary numbers

As already stated, numerology and astrology are closely linked. It is therefore not surprising to find that the zodiac signs also have their own numbers.

Students of astrology will be aware that the first sign of the zodiac is Aries, so we will start with that star sign and proceed in sequence through all **12** signs, including the ruling planet, and also noting whether the aspect is positive, giving forceful, physical qualities or negative, with mental qualities.

STAR SIGN	RULED BY	ASPECT	NUMBER(S)
ARIES	MARS	POSITIVE	9
TAURUS	VENUS	POSITIVE	6
GEMINI	MERCURY	POSITIVE	5
CANCER	MOON	POSITIVE	2 and 7
LEO	SUN	POSITIVE	1 and 4
VIRGO	MERCURY	NEGATIVE	5
LIBRA	VENUS	NEGATIVE	6
SCORPIO	MARS	NEGATIVE	9
SAGITTARIUS	JUPITER	POSITIVE	3
CAPRICORN	SATURN	POSITIVE	8
AQUARIUS	SATURN	NEGATIVE	8
PISCES	JUPITER	NEGATIVE	3

Students of astrology will note that for Pisces and Scorpio only one planet has been given in this example, whereas both signs relate to two planets.

When we have established the life number, destiny number, heart, expression and fadic numbers for ourselves, about which we shall learn later, it may be interesting to refer back to this section on the zodiac, and see how our zodiac numbers fit into the scheme of things.

We should note at this stage that Cancer and Leo have dual numbers because the sun and moon themselves have what are called **double numbers** being interrelated with other planets – the sun is related to Uranus, so we arrive at **1–4**, and the moon with Neptune, so we arrive at **2–7**.

It is also worth noting that many times there will seem to be a connection between the numbers relating to opposing signs, for example, Capricorn being number **8** may well have a link with Cancer, being numbers **2** and **7**.

Some people may find that the numbers relating to their zodiac sign have a special significance or are lucky in their lives.

WORKING OUT FORTUNATE DATES

Numerology can also be used to work out whether you are likely to have a good or bad day. It is useful to have this sort of information to hand if scheduling work commitments, parties or special projects. Writing down your date of birth and reducing it to find your birth number, you can compare this with days of the week and see how the day is likely to go.

Let's take *Paul Smith* again. As we have established, his birthdate works out at **32**, which is further reduced to **5**. The days of the week start with Sunday being day **1**, and go through to number **9**, as Sunday and Monday are **1** and **8** and **2** and **9** respectively. From this we can take it that any gambles should perhaps be scheduled for a Thursday (day **5**). It can also be suggested that his best month would be May (month **5**) and that the **5**th day of the each month may also be fortuitous.

Maybe you can try this out in a small way before taking any major gambles based on this system, but many people are convinced that it works for them.

The meanings of the numbers

In the following chapters we are going to be looking at the meanings behind the numbers found from both our names and our dates of birth. These interpretations are traditional, of unknown history, and despite differing numerology systems, have changed very little.

Many numerologists who work at providing readings on a daily basis may have devised certain modifications to these standard meanings, and this is worth bearing in mind.

What is contained in this book are the standard, accepted and traditional meanings.

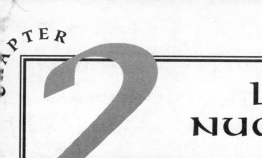

LIFE NUMBERS

*The information we derive from **life numbers**, sometimes also called **birth path numbers** will correspond closely with information we could obtain from astrology, as they are closely related. It is obvious that at the moment of birth, many things come together to make the individual, including planetary aspects and numerological concerns. As with astrology, the life number gives a great deal of information, but you should always be careful not to fall into the trap of expecting everyone to fall neatly into the description provided here for each of the life numbers. Often, people who share the same life number will differ widely. The aims of this book are to show the main, general, characteristics of each number, giving both the negative and positive aspects, and to point people in the right direction with regard to jobs, relationships and likely health problems.*

WHAT TO LEARN FROM THE BIRTHDATE

Found from your birthdate, the **life number** contains advice on how to live your life. Obviously, unlike numbers derived from the name which may change through marriage or for another reason, your life number never changes and remains constant. That is why the number derived from the birthdate is called the life number – it stays with you throughout the whole of your lifetime.

The life number is probably the most important number in numerology, and for this reason we need to look at it in detail.

What you need to know to work out a Life number

Unlike astrology, it is not necessary to have details on place of birth or time of birth. The only information we need is the date. This makes it very easy to find life numbers from friends and family without their being aware that you are likely to be using this information for practice purposes. Perhaps instead of using your own date of birth when practising, you should use the date of birth of someone else. You may find the information obtained as a result more than interesting! In addition, you may not be able to see your own faults, whereas you are probably only too aware of the faults of those around you.

Most systems of numerology accept that to find the life number you should use the whole birthdate. One exception to this is the system used by Cheiro, mentioned earlier. He felt it only necessary to use the date and year and not include the month. This is not, however, the normal way of calculating life numbers, and what we will use here is the whole of the birthdate.

Starting to think about the science

We have already looked at the example of Paul Smith, but let's take another example and look at the meanings of the numbers we get.

Mary's birthdate is 24th November 1963. This reduces to **24. 11. 1963**. Add all these numbers together and you arrive at **6**, **2** and **19**. Reduce this further to **27**, and then again to **9**.

As you will see from this example, sometimes it is necessary to keep on reducing the numbers until they form a single digit. As we have already established, however, the numbers **11** and **22**, being master numbers, are not further reduced.

The meanings of the numbers we arrive at are simple, and are given on the following pages.

LIFE NUMBER 1

ZODIAC CONNECTION

This number is traditionally associated with the sun and with the fire signs of Leo, Sagittarius and Aries, but especially with Leo. The number **1** is the basis for all other numbers, and is often called the **number of life**.

PERSONALITY PROFILE

Number **1** people are the leaders of their community, with a singleness of purpose and tenacity, people who keep going no matter what. Ambition is high in their life. Sometimes they can be over dominating or intolerant; they should learn that they are not always right, and listen to other people's viewpoints a little more. They have strong opinions, a lot of energy, power, drive and enthusiasm, and are generally very positive, independent and decisive. These people are often very obstinate and conceited, and subject to inner depressions which they may keep to themselves. They can be very strong and ruthless in business. They are also highly individual and inventive, liking freedom and independence. They do not have a lot of close friends. Despite the fact that they are very warm and kind, they often find it hard to show affection. They may have problems seeing projects through to completion, and can often take on too much at once.

KABBALISTIC MEANINGS

Totality, unity and wholeness.

EXPECTANCIES

People whose life number is **1** are likely to lead very fruitful lives, following their own inclinations, and being their own person.

HEALTH

They are likely to suffer with heart or circulation problems, and may also have poor vision or eye trouble.

JOB

They should look towards something creative which allows them freedom from restriction and leads to a position of authority, which they will feel is theirs by right.

LIFE NUMBER 2

ZODIAC CONNECTION

This is the first of the **feminine** numbers (all odd numbers are considered **masculine** and even numbers softer and **feminine**) and is the number of duality. As such it corresponds well with the air signs of Gemini and Libra, as number 2 people have a need for balance and harmony. However, its corresponding planet is the moon, which links with Cancer.

PERSONALITY PROFILE

Number 2 people are well balanced, placid, unselfish, sociable, inventive and cheerful, with an inborn gentility and sensitivity. They love their home and family life and are excellent in the company of others. They can, however, be easily hurt and may become depressed as a result. They thrive in happy surroundings. Normally, number 2 people do not possess great physical strength. They often have the capacity to be very devious and underhanded. Number 2 people are ideal in a supportive role, either in business or in the home, as they consider the opinions and feelings of others more than their own needs. They can be relied upon in a crisis. There is, however, a tendency with number 2 people towards inconsistencies, especially emotional, and they should try to balance out this part of their character. They often have problems with responsibility and making decisions, and need to learn to express their feelings rather than keeping them inside, as this can lead to their being rather over-emotional at times. They are naturally romantic and artistic and should learn to be more forceful. They often lack self-confidence and are over-sensitive.

KABBALISTIC MEANINGS

Relatedness, polarity and division.

EXPECTANCIES

Those with number **2** as their life number are likely to find circumstances repeating themselves, in order for them to learn. They should learn to exert self-control.

HEALTH

They are likely to suffer with digestive or stomach problems.

JOB

They should look towards being part of a team, and should consider a job where they deal with people. Many people who are number **2**s find their way into politics. They hold on to any money they make and do not part with cash lightly.

LIFE NUMBER 3

ZODIAC CONNECTION

A creative number, a number of growth and expansion, and thereby associated with Jupiter, the planet of expansion and growth.

PERSONALITY PROFILE

Number **3** people are versatile and adaptable, never satisfied unless they are constantly moving forward and changing. This is the number of the idealist, the traveller, scientist, inventor. They tend to look at everything as a major challenge, are always active and usually lucky with money. They dislike any situation which does not allow them to rise in the world, and have a love of order and discipline. Number **3** people are usually very good company, free with praise but not always realistic. Humour plays a large part in their life, and they have an inherent literary ability and gift with words. They are natural charmers, who seem to be totally without worries. They need to balance their natural extravagance and gaiety at times, and this, together with the inability to think of others, is something they should watch. They can be extremely bossy, impatient and indifferent to others' viewpoints. They should avoid becoming conceited or boastful, which often gives them bitter enemies.

KABBALISTIC MEANINGS

Completion, manifestation and fertility. It is also worth noting that Pythagorus considered **3** to be the perfect number.

EXPECTANCIES

As the number **3** is often considered to be lucky, it follows that people whose life number is **3** are likely to have fortunate and happy lives. They tend to travel and learn a lot from their experiences. However, they often lack confidence and find it hard to form long-lasting relationships.

HEALTH

They are likely to suffer from nervous problems due to overwork. Problems such as sciatica or skin complaints are also common for number **3** people.

JOB

They need to have freedom and will often be best suited to a job which allows them the freedom to travel, but which also has potential. They will not be confined or restricted under any circumstances. They need to have a sense of authority and often do well in government or in the military.

LIFE NUMBER 4

ZODIAC CONNECTION

This is an earth number, associated with the signs of Taurus, Virgo and more especially with Capricorn, and as such, these people can be very materialistic, hard-working, yet loyal and devoted to their families. In a planetary sense, number 4 links with Uranus. Some modern numerologists link the number 4 to the sun, but I would dispute this theory. It also has connections with Aquarius.

PERSONALITY PROFILE

Number 4 people are hard-working, sensible, logical, needing stability and security to operate effectively. They will stick to a course of action through thick and thin, are extremely loyal and practical and are dedicated to charitable causes. They often seem to have to struggle just to survive, and can also appear to be opposed to everyone around them, always taking the opposite view to that which is expected. Able to learn from their mistakes, they are good statisticians and anything systematic appeals to them. They respect law and order, routine and practicality, and are very thorough in all they undertake. However, they are also very clumsy by nature. They rarely make a fortune in their lifetimes. Number 4 people are often seen to be the rebels in our midst, especially when confronted by the underdog. They rarely seem to panic, and are often thought of as dull. One of their problems is that they dislike making changes in their own lives and can be rather stubborn, over-serious and set in their ways. They often need to be more flexible and try new ideas. Melancholy and depression often strike number 4 people, and they are essentially lonely people with few friends. However, they have a natural affinity with number 8 people, both numbers being linked to fate and destiny, and an empathy with number 1 people. Often numerologists will write 1–4 or 4–1 for people who are number 1s or number 4s because of the close relationship between these numbers and the close harmony between Uranus (4) and the Sun (1). It should be realised, however, that number 4 people are very much individualists, and therefore will not be ruled by number 1 people.

KABBALISTIC MEANINGS

Law, reliability and solidity, the solidity of the earth (this being an earth number) being suggested by the four cardinal points (north, south, east, west) and the four elements (air, earth, fire, water).

EXPECTANCIES

People with number **4** as their life number are likely to be popular, with many friends in their lifetime, and often are very successful in the material world. They need to learn to be a little more adventurous at times, and deviate from the traditional path.

health

They are likely to suffer from psychosomatic problems, due to nervous tension, headaches and kidney or bladder disturbances. It has been suggested that number **4** people should turn to vegetarianism in order to reduce their digestive problems. Number **4** people often respond well to hypnosis, which would help them with the stress from which they suffer and the tensions they frequently feel.

JOB

They are best suited to something constructive and methodical, making excellent builders, architects and designers, often in traditional and large organisations. They make good reformers, as they tend to have very positive yet slightly unconventional views.

Take care   The number **4** is a very strong number, and someone affected by the number **4** would do well to avoid both that number and the number **8** in their lives as much as practically possible, so as not to increase the power of the number beyond the realms of control. An example of this would be to avoid living in a house containing those numbers and avoid scheduling anything of importance on dates containing **4** or **8**.

LIFE NUMBER 5

ZODIAC CONNECTION

The number 5 links with Mercury, and as such with communication and intellect. It is also thought of as the number of Aquarius, also connecting with Virgo and Gemini.

PERSONALITY PROFILE

These people are lively, very creative and artistic, vivacious and energetic, disliking routine and restrictions and needing constant change and excitement, often living on their nerves. They make friends easily, are naturally sympathetic, and frequently have more friends than any other number. They are intrigued by the unknown and unusual. As number 5 is the number of magic, they tend to be lucky, seeming to be resilient to everything. Their quick wit and sense of humour sees them through otherwise difficult situations, but they can also be unreliable and idealistic. Many people who are under the influence of the number 5 have problems with addictions to food, drink, sex or drugs. These people are natural adventurers, and often need the praise of those around them to be truly happy. One of their problems is that they sometimes take on more than is possible to achieve, and may become restless as a result. They should learn to guard against changing direction too frequently and to take responsibilities seriously. They are often far too rash and irresponsible, and may be seen as eccentric and thoughtless. They should pay attention to their nerves and their stress levels, as they are easily irritated when stressed. Being naturally hard on themselves, they readily become despondent.

KABBALISTIC MEANINGS

Regeneration, expansion, life, creativity and sexuality. Kabbalists suggest that the number 5 relates to man by virtue of our having 5 fingers, 5 toes and 5 senses.

EXPECTANCIES

Those people whose life number is **5** may experience many difficulties during their lifetimes, yet win through in the end and live to an old age.

HEALTH

Like number **3** people, **5** people suffer from nervous problems due to overtaxing themselves. They live too much on their nerves, often suffering from insomnia and neuritis, and could do well to learn relaxation and meditation techniques.

JOB

They should look towards communications, teaching, publishing or saleswork. Number **5** people are often successful writers and poets, and, as they love change and speculation, are also successful in the Stock Exchange. They love to travel, and would enjoy anything associated with the travel industry or which allows them to see foreign countries.

LIFE NUMBER 6

ZODIAC CONNECTION

This number connects with Venus, the planet of love (of home as well as in the personal sense).

PERSONALITY PROFILE

Number **6** is the number of balance and harmony (linking with the zodiac sign of Libra) and is also a number relating to health and health matters. Number **6** people know how to balance family loyalties and responsibilities with those of job and career. They tend to have an interest in food and nutrition, as well as a love of nature, animals and children, although they may be careless when it comes to their own health and well-being. Number **6** people are comfortable to be around, seem to have a magnetism and attraction, and are often successful in business, allowing them to indulge themselves in luxury items. They love beautiful things, have artistic tendencies and are fond of music and colour. They often work well in partnerships or in the service of a cause or group. Always punctual, even if they have enjoyed a night-out the previous evening, they are popular employees. Naturally caring and creative, they are often interested in the arts or in conservation issues. Dependable, faithful and honest people, they are kind and considerate, disliking discord. Their faults lie in their jealousy, selfishness and possessiveness towards others, especially in close relationships, their lack of practicality, self-indulgent tendencies, and their need to sacrifice more than is necessary to a cause. They can become over concerned with details and seem fussy or self-righteous. Once angry, they are quite formidible.

KABBALISTIC MEANINGS

Harmony, hearth and home, and fruitfulness.

EXPECTANCIES

Those people whose life number is **6** are likely to find success only when they stick to their purpose and aims. They are likely to have a life of change and variance.

HEALTH

They tend to suffer with their voice, throat, nose and lungs. They are likely to benefit considerably from regular outdoor exercise. In later years, **6** people often develop circulatory problems.

JOB

They are natural entertainers and can often find happiness in the entertainment industry and in the arts. They are also happy in the health field, especially dealing with dietary matters.

LIFE NUMBER 7

ZODIAC CONNECTION

The number **7** is another magical number, associated with mystics and mysticism, seekers and philosophers, as well as spiritual issues and inner reflection and analysis. We therefore need to look at this number carefully. Remember that there are **7** colours, **7** days of the week, **7** planets known to the ancients and **7** notes in the diatonic scale. Sometimes this number is linked with fanaticism in its various guises. Connected with the moon, but also with Neptune, which word itself contains **7** letters, number **7** has links with the zodiac sign of Sagittarius. Bible students will be aware that the number **7** appears frequently in the Book of Revelation.

PERSONALITY PROFILE

Number **7** people are frequently very psychic or gifted in a spiritual way, and the number may be referred to as a *spiritual number*. This is a number for meditation, and often number **7** people will meditate naturally. Highly sensitive, introverted and intuitive, with a sense of spirituality which does not follow the beaten path, they often experience vivid dreams or form their own religious groups. Reading and learning are important – these are the thinkers and idealists of this world. (The statue 'The Thinker' is the essential number **7**.) As they are intrinsically kindly people, they are drawn into helping others, even if it is not in the form of a job. They are naturally wise and Good Samaritans, and will help anyone at any time, frequently at a cost to themselves. Sometimes, they become more interested in the spiritual than the material, and seem distant, or out-of-touch with reality, as a result. Contemplative, and very discerning in their friendships, their strong imagination often leads them to flights of fancy which have no basis in truth. They should avoid the tendency to escapism. They can seem very calculating and analytical but they need to weigh things up before making any decisions. They must have their own space, and often like to travel. Happy in their own company, enjoying silence, number **7** people may be inventive in some way. However, any money they make from an invention is likely to be donated to a charitable cause. They should avoid being too outspoken, especially when the subject matter is close to their hearts, and should also watch the tendency to be morbid and unsociable at times.

KABBALISTIC MEANINGS

Magic, mysticism and psychism.

EXPECTANCIES

People whose birth number is **7** are likely to become very successful and/or prominent. They are always looking for new experiences and opportunities for growth.

HEALTH

They should learn to stop worrying so much, as this affects their well-being more than any other factor. When things are going well, they will be fine, but when things, or other people, start to get difficult, all sorts of health problems will develop. They are likely to suffer from skin irritations or complaints and should watch their diet.

JOB

A career that allows them to look after others will prove interesting, as will anything creative. As a result, many number **7** people are drawn into the world of television or films, or to a literary or artistic career. Travel is also connected with **7** people and may mean they look for a job in the travel industry or one which allows them to travel. Many **7** men will have an affinity with the sea and be sailors, importers or exporters or, at the very least, aim to have a boat of their own.

LIFE NUMBER 8

ZODIAC CONNECTION

Ruled by Saturn, a planet known for endurance and status, number **8** people are often very materialistic, but with a degree of spirituality also. It is a number representing both the material and spiritual worlds, and is considered to be a karmic number, Saturn often being linked with fate. It is also said to be a number of infinity. Number **8** people are frequently misunderstood in their lifetime, fame often coming to them after their death. They often appear to be a total enigma. Number **8** is sometimes called the *Symbol of Human Justice*, and some numerologists maintain that the number **888** is the number of Jesus, as it reduces to **24** and then to **6**, the number of love. Number **8** is said to link with the zodiac sign of Scorpio, the **8**th sign, and also with Capricorn.

PERSONALITY PROFILE

Number **8** people are driven by a need to succeed in all they undertake, and are usually self-sufficient, ambitious and career-minded. They never give up and often succeed against insurmountable odds through willpower, hard work and determination. Stubborn, deep, intense, constant and persistent people, they are able to concentrate for a very long time. They make bitter enemies, often seeming too pushy and demanding. Number **8** people have a natural affinity with number **4** people, and both numbers, to some degree, are related to fate and destiny. Number **8** people are very organised and practical, and have good judgemental powers. They tend to think big and aim big, and make good executives in large organisations. They have an air of authority which, however, often is not matched in reality. They are always in control, and emotionally may be somewhat calculating. Personal relationships can be a problem for **8** people and they often have to endure sorrow and loss more than other numbers. Their inability to share things is something upon which they should work, as they often find themselves lonely and isolated, having achieved material success and self-sufficiency. They should also learn to be a little less blunt and ruthless on occasions; they can seem unbending at times. Tension and stress is another area where **8** people are susceptible. They often drive themselvs far too hard and health problems result. Because they refuse to admit they may be wrong, they often follow a course of action detrimental to their well-being.

KABBALISTIC MEANINGS

Ambition, justice, leadership and material concerns.

expectancies

People whose life number is **8** should be aware that whilst they are likely to have an active life, it is unlikely to be without traumas, due in a large way to temper outbursts.

health

They tend to be plagued by liver problems, headaches, rheumatism and diseases of the blood. They would do well to consider a vegetarian lifestyle.

job

They should look to working in large organisations, where they can climb the corporate ladder, or in government, or some other form of public life. They need an adventurous career, something with challenge and excitement, and always need new goals to aim for. Their understanding of money makes them well-suited to a career in finance or fund-raising for charities. They are natural business people, and would do well to team up with someone whose life number is **4**, as there is a natural affinity here.

Take care   Read the comments contained at the end of the section relating to the number **4**, as they also apply to number **8** people.

LIFE NUMBER 9

zodiac connection

The number **9** is the number of the universe, and is connected with the planet Mars, and thus action, force, energy, drive and enthusiasm. The number is also said to have links with the zodiac sign of Pisces, as well as Aries.

personality profile

Number **9** people are both creative and aware of their spirituality. They are often visionaries, or workers for mankind. Charitable deeds appeal to their sense of purpose in life, and they often spend time helping the less fortunate. They have an inner compassion and ideology rarely found in other numbers, often stemming from a difficult childhood. They are very forgiving people, yet dislike any form of personal criticism, feeling they are beyond reproach. Good at starting projects but often lacking in the drive to see things through to their conclusion, they are extremely honest people who can also be careless in financial matters, possessive and moody. They are quite competitive, and often are hasty as a result, but always discreet, sympathetic and helpful. They need to learn self-control, especially concerning food and drink, as they can be quite volatile at times. They should realise that they cannot always be their own masters, listen to the voice within, the voice of conscience, a little more often, and develop patience. Whilst outwardly friendly and courteous, patience is not high on their list of positive qualities. They often inadvertently upset those who are close to them. Number **9** people frequently feel the need to succeed at all costs, and failure is a crushing blow to them. A period of lethargy will follow a failure. They can be very passionate and easily impressed. Often **9** people seem old beyond their years. They value knowledge for its own sake and are natural philosophers. Number **9** people are often well-travelled.

KABBALISTIC MEANINGS

Inspirational leadership, and humanitarian concerns.

EXPECTANCIES

Those people whose life number is **9** are likely to have an interesting and varied life.

HEALTH

They are likely to suffer from fevers, such as measles, scarlet fever etc. They like rich and spicy foods and fine wines, and would do well to avoid these if they wish to see an improvement in their health.

JOB

They should look towards something philanthropic. Being an artist, musician, writer or working within a religious framework will appeal. They have a heightened sense of the dramatic and may do well in the theatre or in entertainment. They also make good soldiers and military personnel, and, being logical are good advisers.

Extra information   As we have already discussed, **9** is a special number in many respects. Number **9** is representative of man, the material world and physical action. It is also the number of indestructability and eternity. To Kabbalists, the number **9** represents God, but it is also interesting to note that the number of Satan, being **666**, reduces to **18** and then to **9**. It should also be remembered in this connection, as already stated, that number **9** is often termed *indestructible*, and that it is also the number of mankind. Maybe there is a message in that somewhere!

LIFE NUMBER 11

ZODIAC CONNECTION

The first master number, and a number of strength. There is traditionally no planetary ruler, although some numerologists link the number to Neptune. It can also be connected to the zodiac sign of Gemini, as the number **11** itself closely resembles the symbol for this sign. It is important to remember never to reduce this number to a single digit.

PERSONALITY PROFILE

Number **11** people rarely fail in any endeavour, progressing forever forwards. They can be exceptionally determined, and full of principles, but also very selfish in their desires and aims. Never lacking in energy and drive, they will often be found working late into the night, when most of their fellow-workers have long since gone home. These people will take gambles and risks, but they nearly always win through in the end, despite other people's fears for their ultimate safety. It is said that number **11** people are captains of their soul and masters of their destiny, and that the number **11** rules the emotions and psychic mind. They respect authority, and often attain high rank, where they expect others to treat them with respect in return. Good communicators, naturally warm, creative and affectionate, they make good partners and friends, both in a business and personal sense. They need to watch obsessions, especially with ideals. They should also watch their gullibility, as they are easily taken in by others, especially in business.

KABBALISTIC MEANINGS

There are no direct meanings.

EXPECTANCIES

Those people whose birth number is **11** are very special, and always move forward, never sideways or backwards.

HEALTH

They should pay attention to their nervous state and guard against over-indulgences with food.

JOB

They make excellent teachers and leaders. They often do not pick an easy job and seem always to have difficulties with which to contend.

LIFE NUMBER 22

ZODIAC CONNECTION

The second master number, and often seen as the number of perfection. This number has a natural affinity with the sun. Again, this number should not be reduced to a single digit.

PERSONALITY PROFILE

This is the number of balance, and these people will often lead contented and happy lives, although they will know loss and failure. They should guard against complacency. They often seem to have unlimited potential to succeed in everything they undertake, never appearing to come across troubles in any form. They have an inner understanding, often apparent to those around them, and a spirituality which also is obvious. Their faults can lie in their inability to learn and be discreet. They often feel they know a subject fully when they have only covered the basics. They can suffer delusions and be too altruistic for their own good. They should guard against becoming self-satisfied and conceited. They should strive to reach their full potential, rather than taking the easy course and finishing short of the mark. They should cultivate self-control.

KABBALISTIC MEANINGS

There are no direct meanings.

EXPECTANCIES

People whose birth number is **22** normally lead happy lives and any problems they encounter are almost always of their own making. Bad decisions and bad judgements concerning other people almost always lead to problems for them.

HEALTH

They may suffer from depressions and frustrations which affect their general well-being. At times, they are likely to suffer anxieties but these can be easily resolved with a period of meditation.

JOB

Often found in vocational positions, working for charities or serving God as a monk, nun, priest or vicar, they tend to have no sense of the material world at all.

COMPOUND NUMBERS

Compound numbers are numbers of more than one digit, excluding, of course, the master numbers of **11** and **22**. Sometimes called **secondary** or **spiritual** numbers, they show hidden aspects of a personality.

When dealing with life numbers derived from birthdates, you should always bear in mind the compound number. Likewise, these compound numbers should be consulted when working out numbers from names. The significance may be secondary but should always be considered. As we have already covered the numbers **11** and **22**, these will be omitted from our list.

Compound numbers end at **52**. Some numerologists suggests that their potency mirrors the weeks of the year and so must end at **52**, whereas other numerologists suggest a more obscure reason. However, by tradition, the compound numbers end at **52**, so we will follow tradition.

Not all compound numbers have zodiac connections, but I have given them where they do.

COMPOUND NUMBER 10

This number is linked to number **1**, being **1 + 0**. Adding a zero to any number gives it more power. Obviously **10** is greater than **1**, and **100** greater than **10**, and so on. Number **10** is considered to be a number of faith, completion, fulfilment and attainment. The number **10** was considered by the Kabbalists to be a reaffirmation of the power of the number **1**. Number **10** people are normally well known in social circles, for both good and bad reasons, and often achieve their aims, although they may not reach their full potential. Number 10 people sometimes feel frustrated and unfulfilled. Change is a part of their lives, for better as well as for worse.

COMPOUND NUMBER 12

Number **12** is often called the number of sacrifice and emotion. Connected with the zodiac sign of Pisces, it suggests secrecy and the unseen. Often unaware of opportunities and the circumstances surrounding them, number **12** people tend to fall foul of other people's motives, which may not always be honourable. Number **12** people are easily duped, and are often anxious. They should learn from their mistakes and look to the voice within a little more for answers to their problems. Educational opportunities should be grasped by these people. As the number connects with hospitals, prisons and large governmental concerns, people associated with this number would do well in these professions.

COMPOUND NUMBER 13

Not an unlucky number at all, but a number of change and rebirth, often associated with the zodiac sign of Aries. People who are affected by the number **13** are likely to have many changes of direction in their lives, with periods of upheaval and trauma. However, as **13** is associated with power, they are likely to pull through, provided they use their power wisely. Number **13** is often associated with the unknown and unplanned, with explorers, pioneers, the military and inventors, in fact anything new. Number **13** people should guard against being selfish and be adaptable at all costs.

COMPOUND NUMBER 14

A number of movement and challenge, and a number connected with natural earth forces and the elements. Naturally related to the zodiac sign Taurus, Number **14** people are often found working in the arts, writing or publishing. They are naturally good speculators, and materialistic, **14** being considered a fortunate number where money is concerned. Number **14** people take risks, and any setbacks they encounter are likely to be short-lived. They need to watch over-confidence, stubbornness and taking bad advice from others. There is always an element of danger associated with the number **14**. It is a number which demands caution.

COMPOUND NUMBER 15

Often considered to be a magical number, it is said to have esoteric connections, a connection with the planet Saturn and to be very lucky and fortunate, with an element of power. It is associated with those people who are good with words, either written or spoken. Often **15** people will also possess an interest or talent in music and the arts. They tend to make their presence felt – they are people with a certain magnetism and charisma. They are happy people who often bring out the best in others. However, many numerologists will stress the belief that number **15**, if used incorrectly, can also be the number of 'black magic' or of things which are allowed to get out of hand. As **15** is a dramatic number, a

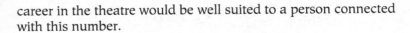
career in the theatre would be well suited to a person connected with this number.

COMPOUND NUMBER 16

C onnected with fate, this is not always considered to be a fortunate number, and is best when related back to the single digit of **7**, which suggests a need to listen to the inner voice, to note dreams, to follow the advice of hunches and intuition. Those people who are connected to the number **16** are likely to lead happier lives if they remain in a supportive role in life, rather than aiming to be dominant. The number **16** warns that events will never go according to plan. It is a passionate number which can be beneficial or volatile. People affected by this number are often rash and impulsive, frequently drawn to exploring and inventing.

COMPOUND NUMBER 17

A spiritual number, connected with **8** and the **8**-pointed Star of Venus, and also with the zodiac sign of Gemini. **17** is often called the number of immortality, of faith, hope and charity, and people affected by this number tend to be well-remembered after their death. They may not have had an easy path, but will have risen above the odds to succeed, spiritually as well as materially. Connected with intuition and consistency, these people are often great thinkers, as well as great doers. As it reduces to the single digit of **8**, which in turn has a connection with the number **4**, the main significance should always be given to the single digit.

COMPOUND NUMBER 18

A very materialistic number, but also connected with the spiritual, it links with the zodiac sign of Cancer. The emphasis for number **18** always seems to be the struggle to balance materialism and spirituality successfully. People who are affected by the number **18** are likely to have difficult lives, with many upheavals, both personal and professional. People affected by the number **18** do not often have a happy family life. It warns of deception, and is associated with making money at the expense of others. It also relates to elemental dangers, such as floods or earthquakes. The number **18** is a number which demands care, caution and love. By turning hatred into love, the problems associated with this number will be nullified.

COMPOUND NUMBER 19

A good number, associated with the sun, and the zodiac sign of Leo. A victorious number, one of happiness, good humour, a charitable attitude and success. It is a very promising number, and those who are affected by the number **19** are likely to lead rewarding and happy lives, often finding recognition for their work. It is favourable when connected with speculation and those affected by this number are likely to be very good with children.

COMPOUND NUMBER 20

This is the number of new plans, projects and actions, linking with the moon, fate and spiritual effort. Delays may dog the steps of a person affected by this number, and there are likely to be many ups and downs, but life will never be dull or boring. Patience is something which should be acquired by **20** people; they should expect the unexpected and not let traumas affect them. It is a number which suggests a need to turn to the spiritual aspect of life to find complete fulfilment and happiness. Number **20** people are unlikely to find wealth but money is likely to be of little importance to people affected by this number.

COMPOUND NUMBER 21

A number of achievement, power and success, ruled by the sun. People affected by the number **21** will rise in status, achieve material success, and be very determined. They may have to try long and hard to achieve their aims, but achieve them they will, because they have an inherent perseverence, and learn from their mistakes. The number is often associated with karmic rewards and spiritual success.

COMPOUND NUMBER 23

A nother karmic reward number. People affected by the number 23 will achieve much within their lifetimes, often with the help of others. It is thought that number 23 people have a special protection around them. Often associated with the Royal Star of the Lion, it is said that nothing untoward will affect these people.

COMPOUND NUMBER 24

A nother fortunate number, one of love, money and creativity. People affected by this number will achieve their aims, have happy relationships and be blessed with a personal magnetism and charisma. However, they need to guard against complacency, selfishness, promiscuity, or any other form of over-indulgence.

COMPOUND NUMBER 25

A strong number. People affected by the number 25 are observant and analytical, gaining spiritual wisdom as a result. They are not naturally lucky people and often have a difficult childhood, but they have good judgement and succeed in the end.

COMPOUND NUMBER 26

A number of partnerships. Partnerships, both personal and professional will always play a major part in the life of anyone affected by this number. It is a number of diversities; it can suggest successful partnerships but also unsuccessful alliances. Many numerologists will suggest that people affected by this number should tread carefully in life, and watch relationships above all else. People connected with the number 26 should beware of extravagancies, as they are often generous people who have little put aside for their own personal needs.

COMPOUND NUMBER 27

A n intellectual number of power and strength. People connected with the number 27 are likely to achieve much in their lives, be creative, imaginative and original. As it suggests that rewards will follow on from hard work, it is sometimes associated with karma.

COMPOUND NUMBER 28

A number of trust. People affected by the number **28** are likely to be successful only to find they ultimately lose out because they have trusted someone or something else, rather than rely on their own judgement or skill. Often associated with the law and loss, it is a number which suggests a permanent battle for security. Number **28** people should be cautious and patient, and trust only themselves.

COMPOUND NUMBER 29

A number of trial, tribulation, treachery and deception. A number which is heavily linked to karma. People affected by this number are likely to have to endure many hardships, both personal and financial. Friendships are likely to be problematic, especially those with the opposite sex.

COMPOUND NUMBER 30

This is the number of the loner – someone who is by nature introspective, meditative and idealistic. The person affected by this number is likely to be viewed by others as slightly eccentric or odd, because he prefers his own company to that of others, dislikes crowds and social gatherings, and has no materialistic leanings whatsoever. This number is often connected with the philosopher or writer. It can be a powerful number. The trick comes in using that power wisely.

COMPOUND NUMBER 31

A number with similar qualities to number **30**, the number **31** is often connected with genius or high intellectual capabilities. The person affected by the number **31** is likely to be even more of a loner than the person affected by number **30**. It is often considered the number of the recluse. Number **31** people have a high sensitivity to the world of nature, and can be rather outspoken and hold fixed ideas.

COMPOUND NUMBER 32

A number of communication, with magical connotations. People affected by the number **32** will be naturally charming, likely to be easily swayed by the opinion of others. They would do well to stick to their guns no matter what, as following a course of action suggested by others will invariably lead to losses. Number **32** people work well under pressure and to deadlines, so make popular authors as far as publishers are concerned.

COMPOUND NUMBER 33

Related closely to the number **24**, this number holds similar meanings. However, success is more likely and partnerships fortunate. The person connected to the number **33** is likely to be exceptionally lucky, as the number **3** is in itself lucky, and two **3**s are therefore doubly so. However, they should guard against over-confidence when things are going well.

COMPOUND NUMBER 34

This links with the number **25**.

COMPOUND NUMBER 35

This links with the number **26**.

COMPOUND NUMBER 36

This links with the number **27**.

COMPOUND NUMBER 37

A favourable number, especially in romantic matters, partnerships and friendships. People affected by the number **37** will be naturally attracted to the arts. They are naturally magnetic, charming and sexy, but sometimes volatile in a close relationship.

COMPOUND NUMBER 38

This links with the number **29**.

COMPOUND NUMBER 39

This links with the number **30**.

COMPOUND NUMBER 40

This links with the number **31**.

COMPOUND NUMBER 41

This links with the number **32**.

COMPOUND NUMBER 42

This links with the number **24**.

COMPOUND NUMBER 43

Not a good number. It is often considered to be the number of anarchy, revolution and unrest. It is also a number of failure and disappointment.

COMPOUND NUMBER 44

This links with the number **26**.

COMPOUND NUMBER 45

This links with the number **27**.

COMPOUND NUMBER 46

This links with the number **37**.

COMPOUND NUMBER 47

This links with the number **29**.

COMPOUND NUMBER 48

This links with the number **30**.

COMPOUND NUMBER 49

This links with the number **31**.

COMPOUND NUMBER 50

This links with the number **32**.

COMPOUND NUMBER 51

The number of the military, the warrior, the fighter. This number suggests success and achievement, no matter what. People affected by this number would do well in the services, whether the army, airforce or navy, or as leaders of people. It is considered to be a number of wisdom, yet also suggests enemies and danger.

COMPOUND NUMBER 52

This links with the number **43**.

PRACTICE

We have now covered both primary and compound numbers. There has been a lot to learn, and maybe we should take a break at this point to practise a few simple examples for John Shipley before progressing to look briefly at predictive concerns connected with future months and years.

- John's birthdate is 28th July 1940. This makes his life number what? I will tell you at the end of this section – don't cheat, work it out for yourself!

- The name by which he is normally known is John Shipley. Using the Pythagorean system, which we discussed in Chapter 1, what does this make his name number?

- If we choose to look at the compound numbers of his birthdate and his name, what numbers do we arrive at?

- Try to think of other things we could, even at this early stage, tell John about himself or his numbers, such as colours, jobs he should look towards, things he should consider improving about himself, lucky numbers etc.

  I am not going to give you all the answers, so try to do as much work as you can yourself on this, before maybe progressing to work out some numbers for your family and friends.

Predictions

We will now look briefly at predicting trends. At the end of the book, we will consider more fully forecasts for months and years.

However, let's take an example of *Mary Bell*. Mary Bell's name produces a number of **21** for Mary and **13** for Bell. Added together, this becomes **34**. It further reduces to **7**. Her name or destiny number is therefore **7**. We do not need at this stage to concern ourselves about what effect this has, we are merely concerned with the number. Her birthdate is 1st December 1955. This becomes **1 + 1 + 2 + 1 + 9 + 5 + 5**. This adds up to **24**. This further reduces to **6**. As her name number is odd, and **7** does not harmonize particularly well with the even number of **6**, we may assume that she will have problems in her life. However, let's now pretend we want to advise her on whether, in broad terms, May will be fortunate for her. We do not have to particularly concern ourselves which May, but we will assume we are talking about the May closest to our present time. May is month **5**. It is an odd number. As her name produces an odd number, irrespective of the fact that her birth number is even, we may assume that using the name Mary Bell, May will be fortunate for her.

A more detailed and precise answer will be found by using the destiny number, about which we will learn in the next chapter; at the end of the book we will look in detail at future trends. However, I hope that from this short example, you can see that numerology can be used in a predictive way.

Thinking of moving?

Maybe we should be aware that names of towns and places can also be converted into numbers, and so we could find out whether certain places would be fortunate for Mary or not. Let's take London as an example. London's numbers are $3 + 6 + 5 + 4 + 6 + 5$. Added together, this makes a total of **29**. This further reduces to **11**. London really is a special place! However, it also produces an odd number, so Mary is likely to like London and be specially fortunate there.

You can try to work out street names, districts, states, counties, nations and all sorts of different places using the numerology system, and by referring them to the numbers produced by the names, see if they are fortunate for you or not. You can do the same with prospective employers' names or the names of firms.

There really are innumerable things you can do with the information we have learnt already, and in the next chapter we will continue to learn a little more about names.

Before we finish, however, I must tell you the answer to the questions on John Shipley. His life numbers are **31** (compound) and **4** as a single digit. His name number is **60**, which reduces to **6**, there are being no compound number for **60**. The rest of the answers I will leave you to find!

3 NAME & EXPRESSION NUMBERS

We will now start to learn about **name numbers**, also called **destiny numbers**, and in Victorian texts **personality numbers**. We will be dealing with names in the next two chapters.

However, before we start to look at names, we are going to take a very brief look at the link between the numbers **3**, **6** and **9**, as there are interesting things to discover.

The 3, 6, 9 CONNECTION

Many numbers have a connection or link. We have briefly discussed compatibility links between the numbers **1** and **4**, for example, and seen how the numbers **4** and **8** are so powerful that they need to have some of their power negated by different numbers, and should, where possible, not have their powers increased. People whose birth numbers are **4** or **8**, as they cannot be changed, for instance, may wish to think about changing their names if their name also produces a **4** or **8**. Using a name to produce a fortunate number, such as **1**, **3**, **5** or **6** make their lives a whole lot easier.

However, let's start to think about the numbers **3** and **6** in particular, and their link with the number **9**.

We have also already discussed much about the number **9**, the number of eternity, mankind, Satan, and indestructibility. However, it is an exceptionally strong number, and warrants further attention.

One thought we may wish to consider at this point in the history of the world is that, on the basis that the number **9** represents mankind as well as eternity and indestructibility, we may perhaps also assume that mankind, too, can never be destroyed.

There are many calculations involving the number **9**, some of which have already been discussed, but to understand this powerful number fully, you must also look at the numbers of **3** and **6** and see how they interrelate.

We know from what we have already discussed that the number **6** is the number related to love, related to the planet Venus, and that the number **9** is the number of conflict, related to the planet Mars, sometimes called The God of War.

Many books, stories, poems and songs have been written over the decades about the power of love, and many set out specifically to tell of love as it battles against conflict. It is often said that the power of love is the strongest force within the universe, and it is interesting to see that when adding together the numbers **6** for love and **9** for conflict, you arrive at **15**, often called by Kabbalists the **number of magic**, which reduces to **6**. It is also interesting to see that using the Pythagorus system for transferring letters into numbers, the actual number arrived at for the word *love* is **18**, which further reduces to **9**, the number of indestructibility! Using the Kabbalistic system, the word *love* works out at **21**, which reduces to **3**, and we all know that $3 \times 3 = 9$, and that $3 + 3 = 6$.

There are many aspects of these numbers which could be examined at this point, but this book does not really allow room for their discussion. However, it is hoped that this train of thought will encourage you to consider further studies into numerology after reading this book.

Names and numbers

Life numbers, about which we learnt in the previous chapter, are always more prominent than the numbers derived from the name, and it is for this reason that so much emphasis has already been placed on learning about them.

Name numbers are sometimes termed as having secondary significance, as it is easy to change a name, but impossible to change a birthdate. In most cases, the name we have is chosen for us by another; and we may decide we do not like our name in some way and decide to change it. That does not mean, however, that names should be ignored. They need to be taken into account to produce a rounded picture of a personality, in the same way as looking at a person's star sign will not give a complete picture of their lives – you have to do a full natal chart.

It is also worth noting, before we start discussing names, that some numerologists will not include **expression numbers** or **heart numbers** in their calculations, looking only at the **destiny number** produced by the whole name. This, I feel, leads to a narrow perspective.

Ðow to start

We have already seen the ways in which the letters can be transferred into numbers, and you may like to turn back to Chapter 1 and copy out whichever system you are intending to use. As I have already said, I am predisposed to using the Pythagorus system, and throughout this text all worked examples will use this system.

When I first started to learn about numerology, I copied out the Pythagorus system on to a piece of paper, and kept it with me to use when working out name numbers. Really, the Pythagorus system is exceptionally easy to remember anyway. All you have to do is to write out the numbers from **1** through to **9**, and underneath in rows, write the letters of the alphabet, starting with the letter A. Should you have decided to use the Kabbalistic system, however, it is a little more difficult to remember, and copying it out will probably be best.

Getting underway

You should by this stage have mastered how to turn a name into a single digit number. However, we will practise one more time, and then move on to break down names into **expression numbers** (using the consonants), which show how others see you. In the next chapter we will break this down even further, to include **heart numbers** (using the vowels), which show how you feel inside, before looking at the name as a whole and discussing the **destiny number**, or **name number**.

We should always remember that we can use compound numbers in relation to names in the same way as we can in relation to birthdates, bearing in mind that compound numbers only go up to and include the number **52**. However, their significance must be noted.

James Webster is normally known as *Jim*. We know that it is best to work out the numbers for him using the name by which he is commonly called. However, if this produces a vibration with too many negativities, we should work out the number using *James* as the first name, and see what happens. Sometimes it is better to suggest to people they alter their name slightly to produce a more positive result.

Jim Webster works out as follows:

$$1 + 9 + 4 + 5 + 5 + 2 + 1 + 2 + 5 + 9.$$

This makes a total of **43**. This further reduces to **7**. Jim Webster therefore is a **7**. As already explained, the number we get from the name is called the **destiny number**, and gives information on how you handle yourself. We will learn about this in detail in the next chapter. However, we can use this information even at this stage. In very general terms, **7** is considered a fortunate number. Looking at the number **43**, we see that is not the case, however. As the compound number has secondary significance, the degree of misfortune will be weakened, but should not be dismissed.

So that you can see the differences when using *James*, let's look at that now.

James Webster works out as follows:

$$1 + 1 + 4 + 5 + 1 + 5 + 5 + 2 + 1 + 2 + 5 + 9.$$

This makes a total of **41**. This reduces to number **5**. This is another odd number, so the resultant differences may only be subtle. We will see the differences in detail in Chapter 5. At this point, we can, however, see how the two names work out as **expression numbers**. Thinking in terms of the compound number of **41**, we will see that this relates to **32**, and is considered a good number.

TITLES

When working out numbers from names, you do not include the titles *Mr*, *Mrs* or *Miss* in your calculations. The only exception to this rule on titles is if the person has a title such as *Lord*, as in *Lord Jim Webster*, or any other such title. He would be known by that full title on most occasions, other than, of course, to his family. Both must be taken into account, but his public face must have a prominence. Some numerologists may disagree with this, but to my view a public face is exactly that – public.

It is also possible to look at their name both before they received a title and after the title was bestowed on them, to see how their public face and overall persona has changed. Similarly, it is also interesting to look at a woman's name both before and after marriage, to see the differing traits and trends. Most numerologists, when preparing information for a married woman, will require both maiden and married names for this reason.

SURNAME ONLY?

In the event that a person is always known by their surname (some people for example, just do not like their first names and prefer to use only one name), this name should be the main emphasis. Poets, in particular the Romantic Poets, are normally known only by their surname. Whilst some people may know, for example, that Shelley's first names were Percy Bysshe, he has almost always been referred to just by his surname. There are several other instances like this, not just within the field of poetry. Many political leaders became known by their surnames – Stalin and Lenin, for example.

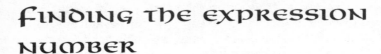

finding the expression number

To find an **expression number**, which, as we have already discussed, is how others first see you, that is your public face, we have to use the consonants in the name.

Staying with Jim Webster for the moment, let's see how that works out.

The letters we use are J, M, W, B, S, T and R. These are transferred into the following numbers:

$$1 + 4 + 5 + 2 + 1 + 2 + 9.$$

This makes a total of **24**. This further reduces to **6**.

Before we go on to see what this all means, let's do the calculations for James Webster. Maybe Jim has his full name of *James* on his cheque book, or it is used when dealing with officialdom. It would be interesting to see how he is thus viewed.

The only difference in letters will be the addition of the letter S. This letter carries the value of **1**. We therefore add an extra **1** on to the number of **24** which we previously had, making a new total of **25**. This reduces to **7**.

Bear in mind these two differing numbers now, as we look at what the expression numbers actually mean. You will see that they produce totally different meanings. Remember that expression numbers concern our public face or image, in other words how others see us.

EXPRESSION NUMBER 1

These people frequently appear to be full of confidence, but this can be to mask their real feelings and they are often nowhere near as self-assured as they outwardly appear. They are natural leaders, and often find themselves in positions of responsibility and authority. They exude confidence and seem cheerfully outgoing, popular, loyal and trustworthy. They often have a large circle of friends and love to be the centre of that circle. Their faults lie in the fact that they can be over-demanding, pushy and arrogant. They should watch this aspect of themselves, as often people take a dislike to them when this side of their character is shown.

EXPRESSION NUMBER 2

These people like to be supportive to others, to live in harmony, disliking any form of discord, and strive for perfection in all aspects of their lives. Unfortunately, however, this can lead them to being somewhat over-critical of others, and make them very difficult to live with. They are quite happy to be part of a team, never wishing to aspire to leadership. However, they need to work on the emotional side of their lives, and allow others to go wrong occasionally, learning to trust in other people a little more.

EXPRESSION NUMBER 3

These people are very cheerful, popular, sociable and confident. Often they will go out of their way to become the centre of attention, because deep down they are lonely. They can be exceptionally extravagant in the way they act, dress and behave. They are natural actors, and love the opportunity to be 'centre stage'. They have abundant energy, can often seem conceited and boastful, but underneath are really very soft and sensitive. They rarely have more than a handful of close friends.

EXPRESSION NUMBER 4

Reliability is the key word for these people. They are loyal, dependable, trustworthy, and very good partners. Sometimes they are very traditional, disliking change and anything remotely innovative, and appearing to be boring and mean. In marriage, they rarely stray. They abhor people whose morals they consider to be lax. They should try to be less conservative in both behaviour and dress, and learn to be more relaxed about life.

EXPRESSION NUMBER 5

These people are full of energy, naturally inquisitive, witty, restless and well-read. They know a lot about a lot of things, but also carry this on to make it their business to know a lot about other people, including friends and neighbours. If you want to know anything about anybody, consult these people, as they are sure to know, and if they don't they will surely find out! They are great to have around, and make fun companions and good friends. However, they seem to have a wanderlust and are always on the move, both at home and abroad.

EXPRESSION NUMBER 6

This is the number we worked out for Jim Webster, using the name *Jim*, rather than *James*. These people are naturally friendly and outgoing. Sometimes considered irresponsible because of their easy-going attitude to life, they dislike discord in their lives, and will go to the ends of the earth to avoid problems. Given an option, they will always choose the easy route. They value beauty in their surroundings, like luxuries and will often have an interest in the theatre. They are the kind of people who will know the difference between a good wine and one which is not so good. They can be extremely charming companions. However, they can also be selfish, and this is something they should watch.

EXPRESSION NUMBER 7

This is the number we worked out for James Webster using his full name, *James*. Often considered to be a loner or outsider, these people are extremely reserved and can seem to be wise beyond their years. They can be very difficult to get to know. However, once you break through the ice, you find someone who is warm, friendly and interesting. Anything slightly mystic or mysterious will appeal to them, and they are likely to be a mine of information on anything of this kind. Unfortunately, other people often see them as introverted and rude, because they seem to repel any friendships offered to them in the initial stages. However, if you really want to make a friend of these people, you will not be disappointed.

EXPRESSION NUMBER 8

Full of energy and drive, determined but demanding, the fault with these people lies in the fact that they can be exceptionally bossy, and exude an air of superiority which upsets others. They are very successful in business, but are seldom liked because of what is seen to be their attitude. Being very materialistic, they value money greatly. They are good employers, probably because they realise the need for financial security, and will be good at organising. If you are looking for a person to arrange an office outing, look no further than these people. They will revel in the challenge, and you can be sure that things will go smoothly.

EXPRESSION NUMBER 9

Charming, magnetic, sexy and dynamic are the key words for these people. They are a bundle of fun and energy. They may not be true beauties, but they have an attraction which is hard to define. They often have many relationships, and also can have many affairs within a permanent relationship. They dislike any form of restriction and are exceptionally bad time-keepers, turning up an hour late for an evening meal and wondering what all the fuss is about. However, they merely turn on the charm, and all is forgiven. They are normally very honest. If they dislike something, or someone, they will say so. You always know where you stand with them, but sometimes they can seem very rude and brash as a result.

EXPRESSION NUMBER 11

This, as we have already established, is a **master number**, and as such is not reduced further. These people are idealists, who stick to their principles no matter what. As a result, they often seem totally unbending, and can make enemies of people without intending to. If you happen to be in their team, you must agree with them to the letter. Failure to do so will result in you being thrown out of the group. They do not make friends easily and can often seem aloof. They are very good leaders, but do not come across as being approachable. However, as with the number 7, if you persist long and hard enough, you will find them exceptionally loyal and faithful friends.

EXPRESSION NUMBER 22

This is the other **master number**. These people have an understanding and innocence which seems unearthly. They are, as a result, exceptionally attractive, with an inner strength which defies description. People tend to look to them for advice, as well as for help, and it is always freely given. They are wise by nature, and can often make correct judgements about individuals within a couple of minutes of meeting them. They are happy people, and are exceptionally valued friends.

CHANGING NAMES

You will see from these definitions that *Jim* Webster projects a better public face than *James* Webster will ever do. Perhaps it is for this reason that he always refers to himself as *Jim*. However, had this not been the case, and having worked out Jim's life number from his date of birth, his heart number from the vowels contained in his name and the destiny number from the whole of his name, and concluded that there was disharmony which could be corrected by altering his name in some way, where would we begin to advise Jim?

Some people have two given names or Christian names. If Jim had a middle name, which, when used in calculations produced a better outcome, maybe he should be advised to use both names. This would obviously be easier, for example, if we were dealing with someone called *Mary* whose middle name was *Jane*. We could either advise her to start calling herself *Mary-Jane*, or suggest she calls herself *Marie*. However, another alternative would be to advise the person concerned to change the spelling of their name. *John* for example could be changed to *Jon* or *Jack*; *Harold* could be shortened to *Harry* or even changed to *Henry* or *Hal*. Making minor alterations like this is far easier, and less costly, then changing the name by deed-poll, although many people do actually do this. I am not referring now to people who adopt a pen-name or pseudonym.

People who have studied numerology may decide to alter their name to obtain better harmonies in their lives, especially those who are about to embark on a career in the public eye. If you are about to begin work of a literary nature or are thinking about a pseudonym, you may wish to consider numerology in helping you to find a suitable and successful name.

fictitious names

With regard to stage names, pen-names and the like, many numerologists feel that, as these are fictitious, they have no bearing whatsoever on any numerological calculations. I would disagree with this.

People who are public figures, especially in the world of entertainment and literature, are very conscious of their public persona. As we have already seen, the expression number is concerned with that face, and therefore, even if the name is a pen-name, or stage name, surely it must be taken into account. After all, it will be a name chosen by the person concerned, and not chosen by parents or inherited from family. It is personal to them, and as such merits consideration.

Nick-names may also warrant some consideration, especially if a person is known by such a name as a matter of course.

The effects of a name change

It must be emphasised that changes such as those given above will not alter someone's ultimate destiny or fate. However, it can make subtle changes to the overall vibrations surrounding a person, and bring about an easier passage through life.

Should you decide to make changes to your name to produce a better vibration, you should start to see a difference almost immediately. However, nobody should expect to suddenly have a perfect life. Free will and choice will remain no matter what, and our own personal responsibility will stay unaltered. Likewise, events seldom suddenly turn from bad to good, so don't be daunted; stick to your new name for at least a few months before making any decisions about the effects the changes have brought about.

BUSINESS NAMES

So far in this chapter, we have only concerned ourselves with personal names. Let's now take a look at business names.

Choosing the name for a new business can be crucial; the name presented to the public can mean the difference between success and failure.

While the full name of the company must take primary importance, reference should also be made to the **expression number**. After all, the expression number is how people see you, or in the case of a company, how people initially view the company.

Let's pretend we are setting up a new company. We have a choice of several names. One of them is *The Diamond Group*. We must, in this case, include the prefix *The* in the calculations.

The Diamond Group produces an overall destiny number as follows:

$$2 + 8 + 5 + 4 + 9 + 1 + 4 + 6 + 5 + 4 + 7 + 9 + 6 + 3 + 7.$$

This makes a total of **80**. This reduces to **8**. When we look at **destiny numbers**, we will see that this is not a bad number. There is no compound number for **80**, so we cannot look at that aspect. However, we do need to look at the expression number derived from the vowels. This could be as important for the company as its overall destiny, as we are dealing with the public image.

Looking at the vowels in the name means we have the following letters:

T, h, ð, ɯ, N, ð, G, R, and p.

These become the following numbers:

$$2 + 8 + 4 + 4 + 5 + 4 + 7 + 9 + 7.$$

This makes a total of **50**, which further reduces to **5**. Consulting what we have learnt about expression numbers, we will see that this number means attention will be attracted, but also that things may be subject to a lot of change. To survive, many companies have to undergo change, so this is not altogether a bad thing.

Whilst most numerologists feel that compound numbers as they relate to names should only come into the calculations when dealing with the full name, let's, out of interest, take a look at the compound number of **50**, which relates to the expression number here. The compound number of **50** relates to **32** and then to **5** again, and is another good number, so things seem to be well for The Diamond Group.

Using numbers for other names

In the same way as we have looked at business or company names, you can adopt a similar procedure for working out the name of a book, play or indeed any other enterprise.

There is a theory that by taking someone's name numbers and birth numbers, and the letters derived from a prospective job, you can see whether all relate favourably. Take the job title of *clerk* as an example. This becomes the numbers **3 + 3 + 5 + 9 + 2**. Added together we arrive at the number **22**, which, as a master number, is not further reduced. If we were dealing with someone for whom the number **22** already had a significance, this theory would suggest that maybe they would be happy looking at a job as a clerk.

PRACTICE

Before we leave this chapter, let's turn for a minute to John Shipley. What further information are we now able to tell him? What are his numbers, so far? Maybe you should make a list, and add to it as we progress through the rest of the book.

I am not going to give you the answers this time. However, take into account any suggestions you could offer to improve his overall lot in life. Maybe you could also make a few suggestions on any lucky numbers he might care to think about, to include numbers we have discovered from the expression number of his name. Don't forget compound numbers!

4 heart & destiny numbers

We will now complete the information obtained from names and concentrate both on **heart numbers**, sometimes also called **desire** or **soul numbers**, and on the **destiny number**.

We have already seen that the number derived from the full name is called the **destiny number**, and that using the consonants of the name, we arrive at the **expression number**. We can conclude from this, then, that the vowels will be the ones used for the **heart numbers**. Once we have learnt about the vowel numbers we can go on to learn about the name as a whole.

What are heart numbers?

Heart numbers reveal how you feel inside, and what your desires are for your life. This does not mean that others will see you in this light. That is shown by the expression numbers. Often people keep their feelings locked within themselves and only they themselves are likely to be able to tell their true feelings. By calculating your own heart number you can begin to find out what really motivates you and makes you behave and think as you do; by calculating another person's heart number you can help them explore their innermost being and perhaps understand themselves better as a result. Exposing these hidden traits provides an opportunity to take a new look at ourselves and make conscious decisions about our future behaviour and actions.

Whilst their relevance again may be secondary, it is very important to remember to determine heart numbers, so let's take a look at the meaning of the numbers.

As before, **11** and **22** are master numbers and are not reduced.

heart number 1

Number **1** is always associated with confidence, strength of purpose and design, and leadership, irrespective of whether we are talking of expression number, destiny number or even heart number. Number **1** people naturally feel they are born leaders, even though they may hide this behind a mask. They have an energy-ratio higher than most, and an ambitious streak a mile wide. They have a dogged determination to see things through to a favourable conclusion for them, and do not take kindly to people whom they feel interfere in their lives. Sometimes someone merely offering a suggestion will be met with a tirade. Emotionally, they take romance and love for granted, being generally complacent in their love lives. They need to exert some of the assertiveness shown in other aspects of their lives where love interests are concerned.

heart number 2

The confident exterior shown by these people is not what lies deep within; number **2** people have a great sensitivity and can be quite vulnerable. They are kind, sympathetic and caring, with a desire to give. Being gifted in healing, they often find themselves drawn to nursing, hospital work or counselling of some description. They need to feel secure especially within a relationship, and they will work hard to this end, as without security their world is unbalanced.

heart number 3

Witty and humorous, apparently never dejected, these people seem to be eternally optimistic. However, often this optimism hides their deep-seated need for love and friendship. Despite their inner wisdom and faith in an ultimately happy outcome to most situations, they fear they will be left on the shelf or rejected in some way. This seldom shows to the outside world, who see them as cheerful and well-balanced. They make good friends, reliable partners and encouraging parents.

bEART NUMBER 4

Preferring to work behind the scenes to being centre stage, these people have a fear of being pushed into the limelight. They are excrutiatingly shy, and very sensitive. They need a happy and secure family life, where they have a place and a definitive role. These people are natural home-makers, and often have the most comfortable and spotless home imaginable. Men whose heart number is **4** are likely to be good at building and capable of carrying out any form of home improvements.

bEART NUMBER 5

These people dislike restriction and authoritarian attitudes in others, and like to go their own way. Relationships are often problematical, especially romantic attachments, yet number **5** people will have a large circle of friends, and feel happy to ask groups of friends round to their home on a regular basis. Often they are intellectually capable of more than they achieve, and may decide in later life to take up a form of personal study or learning. Interested in ideas and philosophy, they are likely to gravitate towards others with a similar leaning.

bEART NUMBER 6

Like number **1**, the number **6** has associations which cross all boundaries. For number **6**, the keyword is always love. These people care about humanity, the environment and the planet. To make others happy seems to be their role in life. They make excellent and loving parents, good marriage partners, and will always be concerned about other people's needs, making sure they are met. Women whose heart number is **6** are likely to want to work from home so that they are on hand for their children and spouse at all times. Often artistic or with literary abilities, these people need that extra bit of praise or support to be totally relaxed and confident.

HEART NUMBER 7

The number 7 is always considered to be the number of the philosopher and mystic. Number 7 people need to know the meaning of life and often have ideas which may be rather obscure. They find their greatest happiness in their own company rather than taking the risk of being ostracised by others, who view them as a little strange, or downright odd. Relationships are not a strong point for people whose heart number is 7, and this is something with which they may feel uncomfortable. They may never truly understand why romance seldom seems to work out well for them. In a problematical situation, they will bury their heads ostrich-like in a book, or surround themselves with classical music to shut out outside thoughts or distractions.

HEART NUMBER 8

These people can be very domineering; they like control because it gives them a sense of security, which, they feel, can only be achieved by their leadership. Number 8 housewives are likely to run their household like a military campaign. They are trustworthy and dependable, loyal partners and often appear to have an inner satisfaction, which may alienate others. They seem unable to relax, however, and even holidays are likely to be taken up by organising outings etc. rather than by simply enjoying the break away. They can often be moody when things are not going well for them.

HEART NUMBER 9

Another number of organisation. Any problems given to people whose heart number is 9 are likely to be resolved without any fuss or comment. They relish challenge and need variety to be able to survive. Naturally restless, men whose heart number is 9 often make excellent mechanics, and are often found tinkering with their cars, or someone else's, at weekends. They have a tendency to want to know the whys and wherefores of everything, relationships included, and this can be a problem in romance.

heart number 11

These people are essentially stubborn, especially where their ideals and principles are concerned. They never deviate from their chosen path, despite numerous attempts by their partners to make them see alternatives. They seem to have an inner faith in themselves. They need to feel wanted, and are often natural missionaries or charity workers. There are times in their lives when they will abandon all forms of security to pursue an ideal, and can thus be seen as quixotic by other people.

heart number 22

Always a special number, people whose heart number is **22** are likely to have great potential and achieve their aims, providing they abandon unrealistic dreams and put in the effort required to succeed. They have a love of perfection, of peace and harmony, and are charming companions.

practice

Before moving on to learn about the **destiny number**, which is the **expression number** and **heart number** added together, let's take a short break to work through a couple of examples.

We are still dealing with John Shipley. Looking back at the numbers we have already worked out for John, let's look at the heart number, and see from this what is really going on inside John.

As we know, to work out the heart number, we are only concerned with the vowels. We are therefore looking at the following letters:

O, I and E.

All other letters are consonants, which we dealt with in the previous chapter. Taking the system we have been using before, these letters work out as follows:

6 + 9 + 5.

This makes a total of **20**. We reduce this to **2**.

John Shipley's heart number is therefore **2**. Looking back on what we have learnt so far, what does that say about John? Are there any new pieces of information we can pass on to him to help him in his life? Remember to suggest that he has **2** in his list of lucky numbers; of course it may be there already. . . .

Ðestiny Numbers

Destiny numbers relate to the name as it is commonly used, and give information on lifestyle.

A point to bear in mind

We have already discussed pen-names etc. and how to change a name to improve the destiny number and other numbers derived from the name. We have also looked at middle names or other names and discussed whether to include them in calculations or not. However, maybe we should consider those people who regularly use the initial of their middle name in their names, as there may be occasions when this will crop up.

Let's take *Michael J Fox*. You may or may not know that the initial *J* in this name does not actually stand for anything. Michael inserted it into his name on purpose. If we were advising Michael on his name numbers, because it has been a conscious decision on his part to include that initial, we must also include it in our calculations, irrespective of the fact that the initial stands for nothing in reality. Consequently, its insertion means that the numbers of the name change.

Should you ever come across someone who uses their middle initial, irrespective of whether it represents an actual name or not, my personal viewpoint is that it should be included in the calculations.

Now, having covered that point, we need to see exactly what the destiny numbers mean.

What are destiny numbers?

Destiny numbers, although often relating to names given to us by others rather than names we have through choice, show how we handle ourselves and things we need to look at, and possibly avoid. Some numerologists refer to the destiny number as the **number of lifestyle** for this reason.

Alongside the life number, it is maybe one of the most important numbers to take into account when preparing a numerological assessment.

Remember when dealing with destiny numbers to refer back to the compound numbers discussed earlier.

DESTINY NUMBER 1

There is a saying 'Look after Number **1**', meaning look after yourself first and foremost, in preference to looking after other people. This number and people who relate to this number, whether by life number, destiny number or any other, follow this suggestion to the letter. Sometimes tyrannical, sometimes just plain bossy, these people will be in charge no matter who or what stands in their way. Number **1** as a destiny number brings the garland of leadership. A dislike to restriction, subordination and being told what to do by others is strong in these people. They will be happy surrounded by people who have a respect and admiration for them as they need to be the centre of attention. Sometimes this can lead to their having large families. They are often creative and should look towards a profession which combines their creativity with their need for space.

RELATIONSHIPS

These people can be quite sexy, imaginative and passionate, but also very demanding. Number **1** people can often be tempted towards affairs outside an existing relationship.

Destiny Number 2

These people are naturally level-headed and well balanced. They create a calming atmosphere by their natural diplomacy, especially in situations which have been allowed to get out of hand. They are tactful and diplomatic, seeing difficult situations through, no matter what, and often succeed well in jobs which encourage these talents. They make good negotiators and middle-men, and are often successful envoys for government bodies. They keep their own counsel, and are very protective of themselves and those whom they represent. Naturally loving, they are also over-solicitous and concerned for their loved ones and family. Sometimes they can seem too considerate, and come across as patronising.

Relationships

These people are tender, kind and practical in relationships and want someone to look after and shower affection upon. They can be very passionate with the right partner.

Destiny Number 3

Cheerful, bright, enthusiastic and creative, these people are good companions and successful in business, due to their need to succeed in all things they undertake. Sometimes disappointments hit them hard, but they seldom show their true feelings and hide behind their natural humour and wit. Often excelling in the acting profession, or a job which puts them in full view of the audience, they can be loved by the masses but lonely in a personal sense. This number is the number of the performer who leaves the stage to go home to an empty flat. They need to feel free, but they also need to feel loved, and often those people who are not surrounded by attention in their working lives will spend their social time looking for someone to share their lives with.

Relationships

A natural charmer is the number 3 person, whose sense of humour is often displayed within a loving relationship. Number 3 people can be quite flirtatious and sometimes long-term relationships lack the sparkle and excitement they need.

DESTINY NUMBER 4

Number **4** people are efficient, organised, systematic and methodical, never wasting time, and are often seen making lists of things to fill the day. Prospective employers would do well to employ these people, especially if they are looking to update or upgrade their office in some way. Leave it to the number **4** person. You will never find them sitting chatting by the coffee machine, as there will be too much to be done, and they dislike gossip. Often people whose destiny number is **4** will be single throughout the whole of their lifetime, seeming to prefer pets to partners, or just being involved in a wide variety of community activities which preclude any thought of a romantic attachment.

RELATIONSHIPS

These people are warm and caring, and yet are likely to look to marry into money more than any other group. They can be very predictable and are faithful and solid. However, they often can be a little too caring, and seem to want to control a relationship.

DESTINY NUMBER 5

Versatility, a need for variety and change, and a desire to deal with people are the main attributes of number **5** people. They are good communicators, hard workers, and successfully turn their attention to many divergent spheres. They need this constant variety to be able to function properly. Unfortunately, this also means they can be restless if forced to spend too much time or energy on something which they feel does not warrant their attention. This also applies to people. Anything restrictive will soon be cast aside. As travel goes hand in hand with them, they are likely to move around a great deal and experience life in other countries.

RELATIONSHIPS

Number **5** people are likely to be Cassanovas, and have a string of relationships at any one time. They thrive on the chase and the thrill of it all, and normally have a strong sex-drive. Unfortunately, when the novelty of a relationship wears off, they are likely to go on to pastures new. They hate to feel restricted.

ᎠESTɪᏁY ᏁᏌᏔBER 6

These people have a natural desire to want to make others happy. They are often successful in businesses where, possibly in a self-employed situation, these natural tendencies can be channelled into a money-making scheme. They are often drawn to the theatre, arts or creative professions. They can be hard task-masters, and are often perfectionists, both in a business and personal sense. Anyone who is romantically involved with a number **6** person must always look their best and fit in with their partner's scheme of things. Failure to do so could result in their being given up altogether in favour of another.

RELATIONSHIPS

Number **6** people are naturally attractive, but not necessarily in a traditional way. Faithful and loving, these people often have problems within a relationship because, firstly, they analyze their partner's motives too much, secondly, they worry too much about other things to notice when their partner really needs love and support, and thirdly, a lot of pressure is put on the partner to look good at all times. However, when these difficulties are ironed out, they are excellent partners.

ᎠESTɪᏁY ᏁᏌᏔBER 7

Again, it is important to realise that the number **7** will, irrespective of its connection, always relate to the philosopher, idealist and mystic. It therefore comes as no surprise to find that people whose destiny number is **7** seem permanently to dream of helping humanity, either by working for a charity or cause, or working with people who are mentally or physically disabled. They are excellent in any teaching role, working better for others than with others. They make good and loving partners, but need the freedom to be able to follow their own ideals. Music will often be a major part of their lives.

RELATIONSHIPS

Often good-looking and sexy, these people can be very physical and loving. However, they never seem to totally abandon themselves within a relationship, leaving their partner wondering whether they themselves have done something wrong. Their mood swings are legendary.

DESTINY NUMBER 8

This is the number of the successful business tycoon, or the person who thrives on heavy responsibilities, someone who can seem to be intolerant of others falling short of their own personal expectations. These people work hard and are often more successful than their counterparts because they put in an effort which others cannot surpass. Very highly organised in working situations, they often place too much emphasis on their career and not enough on their personal and emotional needs. As a result, they frequently have strained family units.

RELATIONSHIPS

These people often seem hard, cold and aloof, wanting to concentrate too much time on themselves and their ambitions to be bothered about working at a relationship. They can have several marriages or long-term partnerships, often because their partner feels neglected and seeks consolation elsewhere. If they find someone who can work with them in their business or who has a business interest of their own to take up a lot of time, they are likely to be happy, passionate and contented partners.

DESTINY NUMBER 9

Quick-thinking, these people often make decisions in a split second. Number 9 people are very well organised but can seem impatient and rash. They want the world, and they want it now. They are not willing to wait for people they consider slow or dull, neither are they happy to stay in situations they feel are unworthy of them. They like change and are happy with professions offering variety and challenge. They are exceptionally loyal partners and will be a tower of strength in any crisis.

RELATIONSHIPS

Because they have the need to be in group situations more than in one-to-one situations, these people may have difficulties forming a loving relationship. When they realise the need for personal love, number **9** people are very caring, loving and warm. They are generous partners.

DESTINY NUMBER 11

These people are often associated with television, films or journalism – in fact anything which puts them in the middle of the action. Communication is a strong point with number **11** people, and, being naturally creative, they often make excellent writers and good teachers. They tend to make friends of people in influential positions, and will utilise their friendship should it give them more power. Often people whose destiny number is **11** will command a large following, and, for this reason, make good leaders of the community. They stick to their ideals no matter what.

RELATIONSHIPS

Another group of people who need to learn about one-to-one relationships, rather than thinking all the time of control and power. Number **11** people make good partners when they decide to give time to the partnership, but otherwise they can be infuriating, often concentrating more on their career than that evening's dinner party which was planned two weeks ago!

DESTINY NUMBER 22

Number **22** people always seem to stand out in the crowd, and it is not because of any physical attributes but more because of personal magnetism. They naturally attract attention, and can often use this in advancing their position in the job market. They have great capabilities and can succeed when other people fall by the wayside. However, they know they possess these gifts, and can often take their talents for granted and thus allow them to go to waste. Practical, yet idealistic, these people normally succeed despite the odds.

RELATIONSHIPS

The natural magnetism of these people means they are often successful in relationships and may have several admirers at any one time. However, they are essentially faithful, and once they have decided upon a partner, they will fail to notice others waiting in the wings. Unfortunately, this may not be the case for their partner, and problems may result.

PRACTICE

We have now covered all the aspects of names. We have looked at the numbers derived from the full name and, by taking the vowels and consonants separately, we have also seen how we arrive at expression and heart numbers.

It is now time to take a complete look at an example, and work it through in its entirety.

As we have already covered most of the aspects for John Shipley, let's stay with him and work it through.

John Shipley

> **name** or **destiny number** = **60**. This reduces to **6**.
> **expression number** = **40**. This reduces to **4**.
> **heart number** = **20**. This reduces to **2**.
> As we have a destiny number in excess of **52**, there is no
> **compound number** here.

Let's take another example, and include within our calculations what we have learnt about birth or life numbers.

Peter Green

> **name** or **destiny number** = **59**. This reduces to **14** and then to **5**. We should look at the compound number of **14** here, as well as the single digit **5**.
>
> **expression number** = **37**. This reduces to **10** and then to **1**.
>
> **heart number** = **20**. This reduces to **2**.
>
> Birthdate = 5th July 1953. This makes his **life number 30**. This reduces to **3**, but we do have to take into account the **compound number** of **30** as it falls within the **52** cut-off point.

Perhaps having looked at these two fictional examples, you might care to actually prepare a reading for these men, to include everything we have learnt so far. Remember to look at colours, lucky numbers, jobs, any suggestions on alterations that could be put forward, as well as to what the numbers we have arrived at actually mean. As there are no right or wrong ways to prepare a reading, I will leave that up to you. However, remember to be polite in your reading yet accurate and fair. Always think about how the other person will view what is being presented to them.

In the next chapter we will look at the other number we can discover, and this is called the **fadic number**.

FADIC NUMBERS

*T*he only number we have yet to find and learn about is called the *fadic number*. Some numerologists place no emphasis on this number, yet it relates to what a person should be learning in the present life, or what may be termed his karmic path.

How to find the fadic number

To work out the **fadic number**, we need to look at the **life number** (i.e. the number arrived at from the date of birth) and also at the **destiny number** (obtained from the name of the individual concerned), and add them together.

Fadic numbers are so different from the other numbers we have obtained that you should learn to look at them differently, and marry them up with the details we have already learnt about the person from their other numbers.

As with previous examples, the numbers **11** and **22** stay unaltered and, again, it is not necessary to refer to the compound numbers produced.

Making improvements

There may be several lessons a person has to learn within their lifetime if the theories behind karma are to be believed. It is up to each individual to decide whether to try to improve their karma or not. Those who disbelieve in karma will obviously opt for the latter. It is essential, therefore, to make this point when preparing any reading which is to include the fadic number, and to also realise that some of the things revealed may be qualities with which the person concerned is not happy to be presented. There are few people, for example, who would like to be told that they have to overcome laziness; they would more than probably refuse to acknowledge that they are lazy in the first place. Bear this in mind at all times.

Let's see what the numbers mean.

FADIC NUMBER 1

These people should watch dominance, being over-controlling, and tyrannical. They are, however, also flexible and creative and value independence. Many people whose fadic number is **1** will have had problems in their childhood and adolescence, finding an easier passage when they reach adulthood, when their aims and ambitions can be met, leading to material wealth and security. They should remember to try to balance the material side of their natures with the spiritual. However, number **1** people will fail to acknowledge their spirituality throughout the whole of their lifetime.

FADIC NUMBER 2

These people are emotional, and over-emotional outbursts can lead to problems for them. Sometimes they are moody to the extreme, and often emotions supersede logic. They tend to be martyrs to other people's whims and views and should be less passive on occasions. Often exceptionally shy, they miss out on many happy times. They can become upset over trivialities and sometimes make mountains out of molehills when situations seem not to suit. They are good partners and very supportive of their families. Their aim should be to realise that other people may not be as honest and trustworthy as they are.

FADIC NUMBER 3

A tendency to be unrealistic is the main trait which number **3** people should work towards changing. They are very enthusiastic and extravagant, and often succeed in business ventures because they are prepared to take risks. They should, however, guard against being boastful and conceited, and being greedy and envious of other people. However, they are extremely jovial people and great company.

FADIC NUMBER 4

E ndurance is one of the main lessons for these people, as their lives will always be full of change and uncertainties. Their caution and rigidity may also cause problems and they should learn not to moralise. They like adventure, and can be quite tenacious, but need to learn self-control and watch inconsistencies, as well as complacency which will alienate others.

FADIC NUMBER 5

W itty, sincere, adaptable and honest, these people will find their lives full of travel and movement. Any period of stagnation will lead to restlessness. Their main lesson is to learn perseverance and to avoid sloppiness in behaviour and manner. Their sincerity and humour are their strong points.

FADIC NUMBER 6

C ompassionate and desirous of harmony at any costs, these people are often also possessive and self-righteous, and at times upset others by seeming to be condescending. They are, however, popular, and have a wide circle of friends. They should watch cynicism and selfishness.

fadic number 7

These people need to learn how to use the many opportunities they are presented with to the best advantage. They should guard against giving up when things go wrong and drifting towards escapism and aloofness. They should use their natural vision and compassion for the benefit of others rather than just themselves.

fadic number 8

The need to learn patience is paramount for these people. They often get where they aim to be, but not as quickly as they would like. They need to watch being over-materialistic, as they may find themselves alone when they leave work behind, having neglected to include a social life within their schedule. They can be very demanding and often harbour resentments towards others. This again should be worked upon.

fadic number 9

These people are supremely confident and go-ahead, and their need to take risks within a business framework nearly always pays off. However, there are times when this is not the case, and they must learn to put money aside for such occasions. They should guard being over-aggressive and blunt.

fadic number 11

The creative strength and stamina of these people knows no bounds. They seldom fail in any undertaking. They have strong principles and can also be obsessive and fanatical. To other people they appear superior and intimidating, and they would do well to work on this side of themselves.

fadic number 22

Always the number of perfection, these people are workers for a cause, and often do so on a voluntary basis. They seem enlightened and wise and their humanitarianism is a very positive attribute. However, they should try to learn to balance their lives a little and aim towards a realistic idealism.

Working with the numbers

We have now covered all the means of calculating numbers using someone's birthdate and name, and practised doing this with examples. Practice makes perfect, and we may now feel we can practise using someone we know, or even using ourselves, provided we agree in advance to accept any criticism fairly.

The aim behind providing information must always be to try to improve someone's overall perspective of themselves. Vast amounts of money are spent by people each and every year in self-improvement and analysis. Often, advice is sought from outside agencies and whilst this help may be necessary, it is also essential to be aware from the outset exactly what sort of personality we have, what makes us happy and sad, what sort of job we would be best suited for, and what lessons we are to learn in our lifetimes. We must learn to know ourselves, and numerology provides the tool to do just that, without having to incur huge costs.

Looking at ourselves

Take a short time, if you haven't already done so, to work out your own numbers. You need to work out these numbers in particular:

> **life number** – from date of birth
> **destiny number** – from commonly used name
> **expression number** – from the consonants of the name
> **heart number** – from the vowels of the name
> **fadic number** – from the date of birth and destiny numbers

What numbers have you produced for yourself?

SOME POINTS TO BEAR IN MIND

- If you have an interest in astrology or know a little about star signs, have you looked at the information we have found from numerology and seen how it relates to star sign information? You should find it relates very well, because astrology and numerology are closely related.

- Have you looked at the numbers, read the sections carefully and seen yourself clearly, not just as you see yourself, but how others see you?

- Have you seen any potential for improvement, or decided to focus your attention on a new career?

- Looking at the section on colours, have you seen that your wardrobe needs more careful attention, so that you have the right colours around you to produce the best harmonies?

- Thinking in terms of the best time to plan things, is there a pattern that you should have tried before?

- Have you worked out any towns which harmonize with your numbers?

- Ultimately, are there things you have seen about yourself which you want to change?

Wanting to change things is most important. If you don't want to do something, you most surely won't. If you decide that the qualities listed for you are all positive, that is fine, but if you see things listed which do not produce that response, what, if anything, are you going to do about it?

Numerology can provide a great insight into yourself and others. You can have a lot of fun working with the numbers and seeing what results, but it is also a science which can be used to provide a happier time for yourself and for others. The knowledge gained can enrich your life, if you allow it to do so.

Numerology can unlock the door to new awareness. You can learn from your own particular numbers when to plan major changes for the best result, when to move, when to change jobs and what to consider, and gain various other insights, all of which will help to make your life a little easier.

By making and considering subtle changes, we can arrive at more harmonious numbers. This must all be borne in mind, as well as the fun element, and the ease with which it is possible to convert letters into numbers and birthdates into something useful.

PRACTICE

Let's return briefly to John Shipley and look at the further number we can work out for him. Remember, his birthdate is 28th July 1940.

His **birth number** or **life number** will be $2 + 8 + 7 + 1 + 9 + 4$.

This all adds to **31**. This reduces to **4**.

His **destiny number** is **60**, reducing to **6**.

Whether you choose to add **31** and **60** or whether you choose to add **4** and **6**, you will get the end result of **10**. This reduces to **1**. This therefore makes John's **fadic number 1**.

Look back over what is said relating to the fadic number of **1**. How would you put this across to John?

It is important to bear in mind all that we have previously seen from John's numbers, as the aim is to produce an overall picture, not a series of fragments of information.

LOOKING FOR THE FUTURE

The only remaining aspect to consider at length, other than compatibilities, which will be discussed in the last chapter, will be a person's concern for the future – what it holds, what should be expected and when events may happen.

As already discussed, the future is not totally fixed, as there will always remain the element of free will and choice. This should be remembered at all times. Trends may be presented, but how we act when these are put to us is an individual response.

In the next chapter, in order to further help John Shipley, and you, we will look at how to turn the numbers into future projections for years, and how it is possible to break these down further.

PREDICTIVE NUMEROLOGY

*I*n this chapter, we are going to take a look into the future, using the power of numbers.

In the same way as astrology is often used as a method of prediction, in the hope that 'forearmed is forewarned', numerology can provide similar information.

LOOKING AT YEARS

To do this type of predictive work with numerology, you need to add the day and month of birth to the year under consideration. This system can be used whether we are looking at future years or years which have passed. It is also possible to look at the present year and work out what sort of year it is.

Let's take an example, and then all will become clear.

As we have been concerned to date with John Shipley, let's use him for our example.

His birthdate, as we know, is 28th July. We are not concerned with the year of his birth. We must add the month and date to the year under consideration.

Let's say we are looking at **1994**. We add together **2 + 8 + 7 + 1 + 9 + 9 + 4**. This makes a total of **40**. This reduces to **4**. John's number for **1994**, therefore is **4**.

It really is that easy! Each yearly number will relate to the period from the birthday until just before the next birthday, at which point it will obviously change.

YEAR NUMBERS

Before deciding to take a look at monthly trends, we will look at the year numbers.

Year numbers go up to and include **9**. On this basis, it is safe to assume that we are all affected to some degree by a nine-year cycle.

YEAR NUMBER 1

This is the start of the cycle, and as with any new start, it is important to make sure that we start afresh, with decks clear and our affairs in order, where possible.

Number **1** is by its very nature an individualistic number, relating to you as an individual. During a number **1** year, you may seem to pursue a solitary path, and have to concentrate your efforts on yourself and learn self-reliance. Many new opportunities will be opened up to you, and you should relish the challenges to be met. It is important that the correct decisions are made.

During a number **1** year, you are likely to find yourself surrounded by new people, within a job or friendship situation, or both.

This is the time to forget the past and get on with the future. The element of change will help remove any unhelpful factors. Whilst at times you may feel that the changes underway are not to your liking, you will ultimately come to realise that things have happened for the best.

Number **1** is also a number of energy and determination, and you may find yourself with extra energy and drive, making you feel restless. Some out-standing matters may need to be settled, and your determination to start afresh will mean such things can be dealt with easily and swiftly. The period from April to November is likely to be the time when new projects can get underway, all uncertainties having been removed during March.

Be sure to listen to other people and not be arrogant or stubborn. It is possible that during a number 1 year, new acquaintances may enter your life to stay there for some considerable time, and it is therefore important that you choose your friendships and partnerships wisely during this year.

YEAR NUMBER 2

During a number 2 year, you should endeavour to hold on to the resolutions made in the previous twelve months, even if things do not appear to be moving quickly enough for you. You should learn to develop patience during this year, in order to establish harmony, which is a trait strongly linked to the number 2. It is therefore unwise to make any major decisions during a period of possible uncertainties.

During this year, you need to take into account other people a little more, and try to work with them as well as on your own. You will have to develop tact and diplomacy at times, as other people have firm ideas from which they will not be shaken, and you may begin to feel that there is a plot against you in some way.

A number 2 year is likely to see favourable health trends, a possibly difficult time romantically, and opportunities for travel. A change of address may also be a consideration during a 2 year, and whilst you can set the wheels in motion, it would be wiser to wait until more favourable trends exist next year before actually moving.

Creativity may run high during a number 2 year, and you may decide to take up a creative pastime which will become very important to you in future years.

Partnerships, both professional and personal, should be worked upon during a number 2 year. You should learn relaxation during this year and also try to hold on to your ultimate aims for the future, even when things seem to be going totally awry.

YEAR NUMBER 3

A year of activity, when you may find yourself more in the public eye than ever before. Many people find during a number **3** year that they reap the rewards for past efforts; it is a good year for business expansion.

Single people may find that a number **3** year brings romance, social gatherings and a lot of fun and happiness. Be sure that negative people do not spoil your fun.

Friendships and partnerships are all favoured during a **3** year, and it is a time when you may decide to opt for a new image. A watchful eye on your diet is likely to be necessary too.

A time of renewed creativity could bring about opportunities which should be grasped, as you should be feeling full of enthusiasm and optimistic about everything. The possibilities are there to have a happy and productive year and it is up to you to make the best of the trends.

As **3** is often considered to be a lucky number, many people will find themselves winning in lotteries or other forms of gambling during this time.

YEAR NUMBER 4

This is the year to get down to business and work, as there is a need to concentrate on material needs this year. A number **4** year is not a year to give too much time and energy to social pursuits. Too much time spent on pleasure will mean things not working according to plan at work. You will want to make plans and lay foundations for future years, and you may start by clearing away things of no importance, and wanting to start afresh.

A number **4** year means you will think in a materialistic fashion and that a great deal of emphasis must be placed on money. It is possible during this period to find that you have extra expenses, over and above those you expected. You should learn to put money aside when you can afford to do so. Financial stability will be of great importance. You may find yourself feeling a little sensitive at times, especially over monetary concerns, and you should be careful that you don't become excessively materialistic or greedy during this phase.

Finding a logical order in which to proceed will be of interest to you; you may find yourself making lots of plans with monthly goals at which to aim. Targets will be important right now. You may also decide upon improvements on the home front. Many single people will find themselves the centre of attention during a number **4** year, as they seek to improve both their appearance and their status.

You may need to watch your health during a **4** year, as well as your finances. The summer months are likely to be the best for progress.

Anything physical will appeal during a **4** year, and many people will find themselves taking a hard look at themselves and opting for change.

YEAR NUMBER 5

This is the year when you may decide to up and move away, change as many things about your working life and home life as you can, and have as many varied and interesting experiences as you can manage to cram in! You will be half-way through the **9** year cycle, and this year could be a turning point for you.

Travel is high on the list of events for this year, and you need to watch your health and make sure you are able to cope with everything without feeling under par.

Any speculations undertaken during a **5** year are likely to be fortunate, and again the summer months in particular should be lucky in this respect.

There are many decisions to be made when entering a period of change, and you may find at times that you have too much to do, and too many decisions to make to function effectively. It is vital that any decisions are thought through carefully, and now is the time to do something to change any element of your life and lifestyle with which you are not totally happy. It is important to stick to your aims and goals at all times and not allow others to restrict you in any way.

As the number **5** is the number of communication, expect to be involved in letter writing, meetings, telephone calls and social gatherings this year. Also expect to find yourself popular with the opposite sex, and have a full diary of social events to attend. For some, this will be the time to experience a number of relationships. At times you may feel as if you are caught up in a whirlwind. You will meet new friends, go to new places and experience new things.

The chance for promotion or starting a new enterprise is likely during this period, as other people will be taking a lot of notice of you. It is a good year for commerce.

As with any period of change, things may not always go according to plan, and it is best during this time to expect the unexpected. New opportunities and the prospect of advancement will be very much in evidence this year. Any setbacks or delays, rather than making you feel restless, should just make you more determined.

YEAR NUMBER 6

Personal matters and concerns are the main emphasis of a number **6** year.

This is the time to sort out any emotional or domestic matters which may have needed attention previously but which were not high on your list of priorities before now. For some, sorting out problems with matrimonial affairs will be the main area of importance, whilst for others, it may be sorting out differences with friends, or resolving legal problems fairly. It is possible that friendships which have been under strain in previous times will become more harmonious.

Sometimes, however, it will not be possible to reconcile all outstanding difficulties, and this is a time when some may experience separation or personal loss.

Single people may find themselves considering marriage during this year, the number **6** being associated strongly with love and marriage. Harmony and balance will appeal strongly, and for all people, the need to feel settled and content will be paramount.

Love will be very important during this year.

YEAR NUMBER 7

This is a period to take a step backwards and allow yourself a period of rest and relaxation. For many, this will provide the opportunity to take stock of events and look at themselves a little more, concentrating on their own health and welfare, rather than that of those around them.

For some people, a period of time away on their own may appeal, whilst for others a need to programme some meditation into their schedule will surface.

Travel is always well aspected during a number **7** year, and many people will find themselves taking short trips away from home. Those working in the travel industry will have an exceptionally good year.

Some travel opportunities may present themselves totally unexpectedly, and these should be snapped up, as should any opportunities for new fields of learning.

Now is not the time to concentrate too much effort on the material aspects of your life. You may find yourself involved more and more as the year progresses in spiritual or philosophical pursuits, and these will be more in tune with you right now.

As number **7** is associated with spirituality, magic and mysticism, expect to be interested in these aspects this year. For those already working in this field, a number **7** year will be professionally very rewarding. Those not connected with such matters may find themselves being drawn into spending time and energy helping others.

·YEAR NUMBER 8

This year will see rewards for previous hard work appearing, albeit a little slowly, but there all the same. Promotion, advancement and progress are all well aspected this year, and for many people business and financial success will become apparent. Romance also flourishes well during a number **8** year, and for many people, this will be a very important emotional year.

This year is sometimes referred to as a *karmic* year, when you reap what you have previously sown. Should you have been reckless in the past, this is the year when it is likely to catch up with you, and for some people, therefore, financial loss and instabilities will now beset their lives.

There will be an emphasis on finances, and, for some, this may mean extra money by way of a windfall or promotion, whereas others may find themselves heading for redundancy or financial problems. Whichever way it goes, the pressures will be great, and responsibilities will have to be met.

Property matters are emphasised during an **8** year, and it is possible that many will be involved in buying or selling property.

Older people are likely to have an important role this year, and many people will find themselves dealing more with elderly relatives than in previous years.

YEAR NUMBER 9

This is the end of the cycle of years. For many it will be a period of reflection and decisions will be made for change and growth, for others it will be a period of consolidation before moving on to new pastures.

During this year, you may find yourself behaving in an impulsive manner, as if everything depends on you making quick decisions. Make sure that you do not act rashly and live to regret it.

Now is not really the time for personal changes. It is not the time to consider moving or changing jobs, however much you may feel the need. Certain other aspects of your life will be changing, and it is impossible to remain balanced when every aspect of your life is subject to alteration.

Now is the time to make plans, reflecting on what has gone before and what has been achieved, and think things through rather than acting.

Anything which has no place in your life will go this year, and that includes people. This in itself could lead to bouts of depression and periods of insecurity, but all this is necessary in order to start with a clean slate next year. Think more to the future and less to the past.

During a number **9** year, think in terms of progression rather than in terms of endings and finality. It is impossible to stay still for ever, and many things which happen will ultimately turn out to be for the best.

Those friendships which are still solid will come to mean a great deal during this year, and it is important that you show how much you value your friends and partner. Beware, however, of becoming over-emotional or over-sensitive.

PRACTICE

We have now covered the yearly predictive aspect of numerology.

Before moving on to learn a little about monthly trends, let's return to John Shipley, who has been with us for some time now, and about whom we should have learnt a lot.

As we have already discovered, in **1994**, John is affected by the number **4** vibration. That means, as we have seen, that work and money are extremely important for him.

How does that fit with what we have already learnt about John? Try to work out for yourself what you would say to John about **1994** as a whole.

It is important to realise that you can also break years down into monthly sections, and we will now look at monthly trends.

Looking month by month

Some numerologists break down yearly sections into three blocks of four months. To do this, we first take the person's age and add it to the current year. This produces the first monthly block. Having done this, we then look at the life or birth number of the person and add the year under consideration. This produces the second monthly block. You then move on to look at the heart number produced from the name and add that to the current year for the third block.

I personally feel it is better to give, where possible, actual monthly details. Those people interested in astrology often expect to be given monthly advice, or in some cases weekly or daily advice, and there should be no reason why numerology cannot provide monthly trends for a person in the same way.

Monthly numbers are found by adding the fadic number (see Chapter 5) to the month and year to be considered.

Let's stay with John Shipley for a while. As we are aware, his fadic number is **1**. By adding this to the month and year we wish to learn about, we arrive at a final number.

Let's say we are looking at March 1994. This is shown as **3 + 1 + 9 + 9 + 4**. This adds up to **26**. Adding this to the fadic number of **1**, we produce a total of **27**, which further reduces to **9**.

We can therefore see that in March 1994, John is affected by the vibration for **9**.

Let's take a look and see what that means. Again bear in mind that the numbers **11** and **22** remain unaltered.

mONTh NUMBER 1

The number of new starts, and a good month in which to consider anything new or untried. New jobs, new contacts, taking on new staff, buying new things, seeking out new friends – all these sorts of activities are likely to crop up during this month. As number **1** also relates to self, it is best to maintain the solitary path during this month and not rely on others too heavily.

mONTh NUMBER 2

The number of harmony, and therefore the number which suggests unions of any kind. During this month, many unexpected events may occur involving partnerships. This can be both positive and negative, so some people may find themselves in harmonious partnerships, whereas others will find themselves involved in arguments and problems with others. In the interests of harmony and balance, it is best to try to deal with such problems quickly and fairly should they arise.

mONTh NUMBER 3

A month of communication with others, and a good month to catch up on business letters or personal plans. It is usually a good month (**3** being associated with luck) and many people may win money in lotteries or gambling. It is a good month financially and professionally, but home life may be a little less fortunate at times. A month to travel, as travel is well aspected.

mONTh NUMBER 4

This is the month to tie up loose ends and get projects off the ground. A feeling of determination to succeed exists in this month, and anything involving legal contracts would be well aspected. Business people are likely to be very accommodating, and it is easier to arrange a loan or mortgage at this time than at other times of the year.

MONTH NUMBER 5

A difficult month in many ways, and a month when the key word should be caution. Many things could happen this month to spoil the equilibrium, and these could include losses. The month has a generally uneasy feel, and health matters should be watched closely. This is a month in which to avoid any legal action, and to take no risks whatsoever.

MONTH NUMBER 6

Depending on which way you yourself act, this month could either by very good or very bad; it depends upon you. Watch your temper, especially at home and be prepared to face delays, especially in travel plans. This month you should learn to count to ten when provoked, and keep counting!

MONTH NUMBER 7

Risks, speculations and gambles will all pay off during this month, providing you follow your own hunches, rather than those of other people. Travel to visit distant relatives is suggested, as are meetings with people who will become good friends in the future. If thinking of embarking on learning a new skill or subject, this is the month to start, as trends are very favourable. This is also a good month for new projects.

MONTH NUMBER 8

Change is all around this month, and there are opportunities for advancement in a career situation. Someone important will recognise your talents and the prospects look limitless. A feeling that anything can be tackled will pervade the month, and anything financial is particularly well aspected. Be careful not to rush, or be too aggressive. Learn to take your time!

MONTH NUMBER 9

A ction is the keyword for this month, and anything which has been slow in developing will take off in a big way. It will be easier to get projects moving now, and energy reserves will be overflowing. Any new ideas need thinking through carefully. An opportunity to be noticed could present itself, and so image is particularly important.

MONTH NUMBER 11

A busy time is forecast but projects will not be completed. This month is a time of hectic activity with nothing seemingly gained, but this is not actually the case, as things are moving behind the scenes. A good month for promotions or anything involving ambitions or new experiences.

MONTH NUMBER 22

B e careful not to be too influenced by others, and be on your guard throughout this period. Any over-indulgences will be costly, as will matters involving the legal profession. Temptations to speculate or take risks of any kind should be avoided, and a control on emotions is vital.

PRACTICE

We learnt that John Shipley's monthly number is **9**. We also learnt that during **1994**, John's main emphasis would be work from the yearly numbers we looked at. As we were looking at March in particular from the monthly standpoint, the work issue fits in perfectly with what we know of the full year of **1994** for him.

If you were doing a full profile for John, perhaps you would work out all the monthly trends individually, and then incorporate important months into the yearly details.

Maybe you would like to practise that before we move on to take a look at compatibilities. By the end of the book, we will be able to tell John about his relationships too!

COMPATIBILITIES

*I*n this chapter we are briefly going to consider **compatibilities**.

As mentioned earlier, some numerologists maintain that you cannot gauge compatibility profiles properly by using numbers. Others disagree. I have formed no hard and fast opinion one way or the other, and maybe further research is necessary on this aspect of numerology.

Perhaps by practising many examples, especially using couples you already know, you will form your own opinion.

how to find compatibility ratings

To find compatibility ratings, you need only use the name. Again, it is the name by which the person concerned is commonly known.

Using the same conversions as used previously, you arrive at the **name number** or **destiny number**. All you then need to do is to do the same for the other party concerned, and refer to the chart, and key.

Let's say, for example, *Beth Smith* and *Ian Jones* are the couple. We are looking at the lady's name as she is usually known, not at her full name, *Elisabeth*. Beth Smith works out at **41** and reduces to **5**. Ian Jones works out at **33** and reduces to **6**. Looking down the women's column to **5** and across the men's column to **6**, we see the number **4**, which means (using the key to the codes) little chance of romantic success.

WOMEN ▶ MEN ▲	ONE	TWO	THREE	FOUR	FIVE	SIX	SEVEN	EIGHT	NINE	ELEVEN	TWENTY-TWO
ONE	2	4	2	1	3	3	1	2	4	4	1
TWO	4	2	4	2	1	3	3	1	2	2	2
THREE	2	4	2	4	2	1	3	3	1	4	4
FOUR	1	2	4	2	4	2	1	3	1	2	4
FIVE	3	1	2	4	2	4	2	1	3	2	2
SIX	3	3	1	2	4	2	4	2	4	3	2
SEVEN	1	3	3	1	2	4	2	4	1	1	1
EIGHT	2	1	3	3	1	2	4	4	2	3	3
NINE	4	2	1	3	3	1	2	2	4	1	3
ELEVEN	4	2	4	2	1	3	3	1	2	2	2
TWENTY-TWO	1	2	4	3	4	2	1	3	3	2	3

Key to the codes

1 = Very good possibilities for long-term relationship

2 = A fun relationship with lots of passion, yet competitive

3 = A clash of personalities, but an attraction, so maybe

4 = Very little chance – too many differences

How do you rate?

PRACTICE AND REVISION

We are now at the end of the book, and have learnt about names, dates of birth and, most importantly, about numbers.

You should also have learnt a little about yourself and those around you; about personalities, good and bad traits, the way things are likely to go in future years and months, and ways in which it is possible to change to bring about more favourable trends.

It is important to realise that nothing can change unless we ourselves want the change, and we must remember this at all times, both when looking at ourselves, and, more importantly, when discussing numerology with others.

Let's return briefly to John Shipley. Let's pretend that he has a relationship with someone who is a number **5**. As we know, from his name, John is a number **6**. That is his **destiny** or **name number**. His girlfriend has a destiny number of **5**, which from the chart on page 95, does not give good indications for the future at all. How would you put this to him? This is difficult. Remember to be fair and accurate, yet also to be kind. Maybe you should just suggest that there may be problems in the relationship and leave it at that.

Thinking more about numbers

Maybe before you started to look at numbers, you thought of them merely as units of measurement or as quantities. It is my sincere hope that you now see them in a different light and that perhaps you also wish to learn more about the science of numerology.

Numbers are more than units of measurement. They represent qualities about human beings and places. They present the opportunity to change our lives and improve; they can help us to understand ourselves and our fellow man. They can be invaluable in social and also business situations. They can help us make plans for the future; they can help us with here and now. We must allow them to help us and to work for us and not work against them.

You may have looked at your own numbers and noticed that certain numbers crop up many times and you may also have seen a few numbers which do not fit in with the others at all. You may have seen, for example, that your house number does, or does not, fit in with your life number. You may have noticed, in the case that it does, that other house numbers where you may have lived previously and felt unhappy, do not fit in, and now see a reason perhaps why you felt uneasy there.

By deciding to eliminate certain numbers from your life, you can make things easier and far less negative. If you are, for example, in the market for a new car, maybe you should also consider the numbers in the registration number. Maybe you should also consider buying the car on a date or at a time fortunate for you.

For many people, looking at numbers shows them ways in which they can help themselves and maybe change things for the better.

Those interested in the reasons for life, the things they should be learning about their life, karmic responsibilities or debts, may have learnt a lot from the section on fadic numbers.

Those people who are in a new relationship may have learnt a lot from looking at their partner's and their own heart numbers, as well as the compatibility chart.

If none of these things are particularly true for you, maybe you have at the very least learnt that numbers are more than quantities.

Since I first became interested in numbers, my perspectives have changed, my awareness of the scheme of things has altered. Everything has seemed more structured and my understanding of human nature has been greatly enhanced.

In the hope that this may now be true also for you, look at the list of other reading matter available on numerology at the end of this text, and learn as much about this fascinating subject as you can. Your life will be mightily enriched as a result.

fURTHER READING

Anderson, Mary, *The Secret Power of Numbers*, Aquarian Press, England, 1979

Cheiro, *Cheiros Book of Numbers*, Ark Books, New York, 1964

Connolly, Ellen, *The Connolly Book of Numbers*, Vols 1 and 2, Aquarian Press, England

Cooper, D. Jason, *Numerology, The Power to Know Anyone*, Aquarian Press, England

Hitchcock, Helyn, *Helping Yourself with Numerology*, Wolfe Publishing Ltd., 1972

Johari, Harish, *Numerology*, Real Books, 1992

Kovacs Stein, Sandra, and Schuler, Carol Ann, *Love Numbers*, Aquarian Press, England 1982

Kozminsky, Isadore, *Numbers – Their Meaning and Magic*, Rider, London, 1985

Line, David, and Julia, *The Book of Love Numbers*, Aquarian Press, England, 1986

Line, Julia, *Numerology Workbook*, Aquarian Press, England

Seaton, Julia, *Symbols of Numerology*, Newcastle Publishing, Calif., 1984

Sephrial, *The Kabala of Numbers*, Newcastle Publishing, Van Nuys, 1974

Taylor, Ariel, Yvon & Warren Hyer, H., *Numerology, Its facts and Secrets*, C & R Anthony Inc., New York, 1958

Wynn Westcott, W., *Occult Power of Numbers*, Newcastle Publishing, Calif., 1984

LIFE Nº

HANS	11 OCT 1950	= 18 = 9		
Cathy	05 FEB 1952	= 24 = 6		
Brett	25 DEC 1983	= 31 = 4		
Matt	23 MAR 1979	= 34 = 7		
Isaac	20 FEB 2013	= 10 = 1		
TENLEY	21 APR 2017	= 17 = 8		
NOAH	09 NOV 2006	= 19 = 10 = 1		
MYA + RIELLE	16 OCT 2008	= 18 = 9		
YVONNE	27 APR 1987	= 38 = 11		
Jennifer	02 JAN 1981	= 22 = 4		
DAVID	02 NOV 1958	= 26 = 8		
VERONICA	11 FEB 1950	= 19 = 10 = 1		
TREVOR	10 NOV 1940	= 17 = 8		